U.S. INTERESTS IN AFRICA

HEARING

BEFORE THE

COMMITTEE ON FOREIGN AFFAIRS
HOUSE OF REPRESENTATIVES

ONE HUNDRED FIFTEENTH CONGRESS

FIRST SESSION

MAY 18, 2017

Serial No. 115–33

Printed for the use of the Committee on Foreign Affairs

Available via the World Wide Web: http://www.foreignaffairs.house.gov/ or http://www.gpo.gov/fdsys/

U.S. GOVERNMENT PUBLISHING OFFICE

25–458PDF   WASHINGTON : 2017

For sale by the Superintendent of Documents, U.S. Government Publishing Office
Internet: bookstore.gpo.gov   Phone: toll free (866) 512–1800; DC area (202) 512–1800
Fax: (202) 512–2104   Mail: Stop IDCC, Washington, DC 20402–0001

CONTENTS

Page

WITNESSES

General William E. Ward, USA, Retired, president and chief operating officer, SENTEL Corporation (former Commander, U.S. Africa Command) 4
Mr. Bryan Christy, explorer and investigative reporter, National Geographic Society 10
Mr. Anthony Carroll, adjunct professor, School of Advanced International Studies, Johns Hopkins University 20
The Honorable Reuben E. Brigety II, dean, Elliott School of International Affairs, The George Washington University (former U.S. Representative to the African Union, U.S. Department of State) 29

LETTERS, STATEMENTS, ETC., SUBMITTED FOR THE HEARING

General William E. Ward, USA, Retired: Prepared statement 6
Mr. Bryan Christy: Prepared statement 12
Mr. Anthony Carroll: Prepared statement 23
The Honorable Reuben E. Brigety II: Prepared statement 31

APPENDIX

Hearing notice 80
Hearing minutes 81
The Honorable Daniel Donovan, a Representative in Congress from the State of New York: Material submitted for the record 83
The Honorable Gerald E. Connolly, a Representative in Congress from the Commonwealth of Virginia: Prepared statement 85

U.S. INTERESTS IN AFRICA

THURSDAY, MAY 18, 2017

House of Representatives,
Committee on Foreign Affairs,
Washington, DC.

The committee met, pursuant to notice, at 10 o'clock a.m., in room 2172 Rayburn House Office Building, Hon. Edward Royce (chairman of the committee) presiding.

Chairman ROYCE. This hearing will come to order if all of the members will take their seats. Today we are going to focus on U.S. interests on the continent of Africa. As members know, this committee has been in the lead of U.S.-Africa policy for many, many years. Last Congress was no different, with several laws passed, and I will just remind the members we passed: The Electrify Africa Act, which will bolster power in electricity projects across the continent, it will spur a lot of economic growth.

We passed the END Wildlife Trafficking Act, which combats the threat of illegal poaching and the trafficking of elephants and rhinos, and we closed down the ivory trade with this legislation. The profits here were linked to extremist groups which was another important point.

The Global Food Security Act improves our ability to respond to food emergencies, and we also successfully reauthorized the African Growth and Opportunity Act to expand opportunities for increased trade and investment.

Not too long ago, the committee fought to establish landmark programs like PEPFAR and the Millennium Challenge Corporation. As this work was done in a bipartisan way over the last few years, we operate the same way today. I would like to thank Ranking Member Engel, Chairman Smith, and Ranking Member Bass for their leadership on these issues.

Africa has 1 billion consumers. That is one way to look at it, 1 billion consumers. It has a huge potential as a trading partner and as a U.S. job creator. Some of the fastest growing economies in the world are in Africa, including six of the top 13 countries that grew the fastest over the last 3 years. This makes our economic engagement on the continent critical. But according to a recent news report, Chinese engagement with the continent "may be the largest global trade and investment spree in history." Simply put: The U.S. cannot get caught watching from the sidelines here.

Our efforts to combat Islamist extremism is not confined to the Middle East. ISIS affiliates and Al Shabaab in Somalia, Boko Haram in northern Nigeria, and the al-Qaeda affiliate throughout the Maghreb have to be addressed head-on through counterterrorism initiatives in support for our partners in Africa. One witness today will tell us about his exploits fighting wildlife traffickers, and many of these wildlife traffickers today are linked to terrorists. Efforts to strengthen democratic institutions and government capabilities must go hand-in-hand with our efforts to address these challenges. Unfortunately, tragically, too many African countries are off the democratic track.

Critical situations require immediate leadership and direction from the U.S. Government. With three famines looming on the continent, deliberate deprivation of humanitarian aid by South Sudan's political leaders, and ongoing political instability in the Democratic Republic of the Congo, the U.S. must remain active and remain engaged. And I want to thank again those members that are traveling to the region in the next few weeks addressing these issues.

I am pleased also by last week's nomination of Ambassador Mark Green to lead USAID. We look forward to working with this former committee member to continue to provide communities with life-saving aid from the American people. AID also helps open African markets to sell U.S. goods and services. However, I am concerned by the delay in appointing an Assistant Secretary for Africa at the State Department, and the Department needs to demonstrate how the administration's proposed budgets don't put the progress we have made in jeopardy.

As we will hear today, our engagement with Africa is in the strategic interest of the U.S. not only to address urgent humanitarian needs there in Africa across the continent, but also to advance our critical economic interests, our political interests, our security interests. Now is not the time to pull back. And so I will now go to our ranking member, Mr. Engel of New York.

Mr. ENGEL. Thank you, Mr. Chairman. Thank you for convening this hearing. And to our witnesses welcome to the Foreign Affairs Committee. We are grateful for your time and for your expertise.

The region that we are focused on today, sub-Saharan Africa, holds tremendous importance for the United States and for other emerging global powers. If we don't give Africa the focus it deserves those strategic opportunities will slip away at great cost to the United States and I believe to countries across the continent.

In recent years, American policy has played a major role in driving political, economic, and security progress in sub-Saharan Africa. For the most part, these policies have won strong bipartisan support. They have also shown good results. Working together we have helped to promote economic opportunity through the African Growth and Opportunity Act, what we call AGOA, and the Electrify Africa Act.

We have improved access to lifesaving health care through the President's Emergency Plan for AIDS Relief, PEPFAR, and through the American response to the Ebola crisis in West Africa in 2014. And we have worked to tackle the problem of wildlife trafficking, which is tied to so many other criminal activities, through the END Wildlife Trafficking Act.

These initiatives are great examples of how doing good for other people also does good for America's interests. If we can help provide access to reliable power or health care we should. It is the right thing to do. At the same time we make these investments we are helping communities and countries become more stable and more prosperous. It adds up over time and we end up with stronger partners on the world stage and populations who view the United States as a friend.

But these efforts, as worthwhile as they are, haven't made a dent in other challenges facing many African countries. For example, conflict and climate change have given rise to massive humanitarian crises including an ongoing famine in South Sudan and the risk of famine in Somalia and northeastern Nigeria. The victories we have achieved are fragile and a lot of work remains to meet remaining challenges.

So I am worried that after robust engagement during both the Bush and Obama administrations, United States' policy toward Africa has suddenly gone adrift. Part of this is due to some diplomatic missteps. In April, Secretary Tillerson invited the chair of the African Union Commission to meet in Washington, then at the last minute canceled the meeting.

In March, the African Global Economic and Development Summit took place in California. Not a single citizen of an African country was granted a visa by the State Department to attend this event. I have to ask, would the Secretary of State brush off the European foreign policy chief? When we hosted the APEC Summit in 2011, how many citizens of Asian countries did we turn away?

Mistakes like this send an unfortunate message. What sends an even clearer message and will do real harm to people across Africa is the administration's proposed international affairs budget cut. If we cut by nearly a third our investment in diplomacy and development, we put at risk all the work we have done to foster good governance, economic growth, and counterterrorism efforts.

And I am happy and I am pleased to say that when we held hearings in this committee, people on both sides of the aisle spoke out against these horrific budget cuts. Cutting USAID initiatives and support for U.N. organizations will put lives at risk. The appalling reinstatement and expansion of the Global Gag Rule will have an outsized impact on African countries, cutting off vulnerable communities, especially women and girls, from needed health care.

Scaling back the Peace Corps will undermine one of our most cost effective tools of providing assistance in building relationships with other cultures. And expanding the American military engagement on the continent just doesn't make sense if we are not also working on a parallel track to address the drivers of political instability.

The good news is that Congress decides how much we invest in foreign affairs and where we put that money to use. We have the power of the purse. So I am confident as we move forward we will continue to give our initiatives in Africa the resources they need and that we will do more to address the range of unmet challenges.

I look forward to hearing from our witnesses about the best way forward on these issues. I again thank Chairman Royce and Ms. Bass for all her work on this and I yield back.

Chairman ROYCE. Thank you, Mr. Engel. This morning we are pleased to be joined by a very distinguished panel. General Kip Ward served as the first commander of the U.S. Africa Command Forces. He served there from 2007 to 2011.

We have Mr. Bryan Christy, an investigative journalist from the National Geographic, specializing in wildlife trafficking and the ivory trade and in conservation.

We have Mr. Tony Carroll, adjunct professor at the Johns Hopkins School of Advanced International Studies. He served on the Africa advisory board at the EXIM Bank, the Overseas Private Investment Corporation, and the Millennium Challenge Corporation, and he got his start as a Peace Corps volunteer in sub-Saharan Africa.

Ambassador Reuben Brigety served as the U.S. representative to the African Union. The Ambassador also served as a Deputy Assistant Secretary of State in the Bureau of African Affairs.

And without objection, the witnesses' full prepared statements will be made part of the record, here, and members are going to have 5 calendar days to submit any statements or any questions that they might have for the witnesses or any extraneous material into the record.

We will start with General Ward and we will ask all of you, if you could, to summarize your remarks. General Ward, please.

STATEMENT OF GENERAL WILLIAM E. WARD, USA, RETIRED, PRESIDENT AND CHIEF OPERATING OFFICER, SENTEL CORPORATION (FORMER COMMANDER, U.S. AFRICA COMMAND)

General WARD. Mr. Chairman, Ranking Member, and members of the committee, thank you for the opportunity to provide testimony on the important nexus between security and development on the African continent and how interconnected they are from a philosophical standpoint, but also operationally between the Department of Defense and USAID in particular but other U.S. Government agencies that promote development and good governance.

Proudly wearing the cloth of our nation, I was privileged to be the inaugural commander of the United States Africa Command, and having previously served in the Balkans as the commander of the NATO Force in Bosnia and Herzegovina and in the Middle East as a U.S. security coordinator for Israel and Palestinian authority. In each of these three critical environs I was able to witness firsthand that American security is well served when nations take and are supported in taking positive steps to advance their economic sector to better serve their populations and inroads are made such that governance issues are advanced in service to their people.

I have submitted a written statement and in it I describe this notion of creating societal stability by providing a horizon of hope. When this happens, fragile societies are less susceptible to the conditions that foster instability and reduce the prevalence of failing or fragile state scenarios easily exploited by terrorists, criminals, and other negative actors.

When the United States provides developmental support to fragile states, our national security interests are served and our national security is enhanced. Development is the long term guarantor of stability. No amount of bullets or bombs can do that. As was the case for post conflict Europe and Asia where the United States made strategic developmental investments, this is no less true for Africa.

The African continent is three and a half times the size of the continental United States with vast resources, markets, and agricultural potential. Population growth in Africa exceeds that occurring anywhere else on the globe. Burgeoning youth populations, huge potential for a rising middle class, and its demands for goods and services reinforce the importance of programs that advance health, literacy, and access to a better life, lest these populations create burdens on other regions of the global commons and, as importantly, create safe havens for the export of terrorism and illegal activities requiring huge resources to counter. Preventing this from occurring is a far better and much less costly alternative than having to react to the negative impact of these ills.

Our national support to these vital developmental projects and programs led by the United States Agency for International Development and other developmental entities are modest investments proportionately speaking that serve our national security interests more efficiently than having to react to crises as voids are created and gaps exist. To make a difference over time we must sustain our engagement—including developmental engagement, diplomatic engagement, and security engagement—over time.

Thank you, sir, and I am prepared to respond to your questions and comments to the best of my ability.

[The prepared statement of General Ward follows:]

Testimony Of
Gen. William E. "Kip" Ward, USA, Retired
U.S. Global Leadership Coalition
House Committee on Foreign Affairs
"U.S. Interests in Africa"
Thursday, May 18, 2017

Thank you, Chairman Ed Royce and Ranking Member Eliot Engel, for inviting me to testify before the Committee today on U.S. engagement in Africa.

As the first commander for United States Africa Command (AFRICOM), I have seen and understand the importance of sustained and meaningful U.S. engagement in Africa. Africa remains and must continue to be a priority for the United States. From inception, and under my leadership, AFRICOM focused on a synchronized approach to development, diplomacy, and defense activities on the Continent and its island nations.

These central themes helped define our interagency cooperation with the State Department, U.S. Agency for International Development (USAID), other U.S. government agencies, NGOs, and private organizations. Under my guidance, the basis of AFRICOM's humanitarian and civic assistance activities were rooted in the notion that such activities should complement, not duplicate, other U.S. government activities, and should bolster our security sector relationships. Development, we believed, is, and always will be, the long-term guarantor of peace and stability in unsettled, fragile, and volatile regions of the world.

As this committee examines U.S. engagement in Africa, it is important to ask what will happen if the United States fails to engage on the continent. Anything less than a well-developed strategy, coupled with ample resources and vision, will signal that America has no interest in African affairs or the actions of other countries throughout the continent.

Already, we are seeing China, Turkey, other Asian nations and even nations in South America fill the void. Africa has a growing middle class and emerging markets, and a growth in population that is surpassing all other regions of the globe. Members of the international community are taking advantage of the changing demographics, to their advantage but sometimes to the detriment of Africa's best interests and those of the U.S. as well. These developments will have lasting implications if left unaddressed. As members of the public policy and lawmaking communities, we must ask ourselves, if the United States fails to come to the table now, when dynamics are quickly changing, will Africa even want the United States as a viable partner in the future?

While at AFRICOM, we focused on "sustained security engagement," which fostered enduring relationships with our African military partners. However, we should likewise look at our development assistance to the continent through the same lens. It is in our best interests to focus on "sustained development engagement" just as we focused on sustained security engagement. Long-term investments in development goes a long way to ensure stability, peace and security across the continent. Increased peace and stability in Africa will help stem the plight of terrorism on the continent, which has global implications. In the fight against violent extremism, our nation's development officials play an important, yet often unrecognized role, in countering the rise of terrorist ideologies.

As AFRICOM Commander, I witnessed the rising tide of violent extremism on the continent. Boko Haram and Al-Shabaab with their ties to Al-Qaida represent critical threats to African regional security and our national security interests at home. However, they won't be defeated through military force alone. Our support to sustained development activities and diplomacy initiative that lead to positive governance are critical in establishing the strong economic and governmental foundations needed to thwart violent extremism from fomenting in fragile states.

That is why funding for the State Department and USAID is so important. Secretary of Defense James Mattis was correct in saying, "If you don't fund the State Department fully, then I need to buy more ammunition." And with all due respect to the Secretary, I add a postscript to his words in that: We can never buy enough bullets to create sustained peace. Sustained stability comes from providing and helping to create a "Horizon of Hope" through our sustained development (economic) and diplomatic (governance) engagement, as had been demonstrated in other parts of the world.

While leading AFRICOM as its inaugural commander, I worked closely with our partners at the Department of State, USAID, and other Departments like Commerce, Treasury and Agriculture to create lasting, enduring relationships with local and regional officials on the ground throughout the continent. At AFRICOM, demonstrating the U.S. military's support for the activities of other U.S. agencies' efforts was important. A guiding principle was to reinforce and add value to the total U.S. Government approach. Synchronized engagement and harmonious coordination between the military, diplomatic corps, and development workers helped transform the U.S. presence on the continent.

This is not a partisan issue. We know that successful implementation of U.S. foreign policy objectives is only possible with close interagency coordination. When AFRICOM was created, the State Department and USAID were firmly established on the continent, leading diplomatic initiatives and delivering life-saving aid on the frontlines and in many fragile locations. One of my main priorities was to leverage their institutional knowledge by integrating senior State Department and USAID personnel into AFRICOM's organizational structure. Previously, the U.S. military had three regional commands responsible for defense activities in Africa. This command distribution neither facilitated a comprehensive strategy nor complimented U.S. soft power. But the creation of AFRICOM allowed for the U.S. military to provide sustained security engagement through a single focused geographic command with our African partners to promote a safe and secure environment across Africa in support of U.S. National policy goals.

Coordination and cooperation with our interagency partners provided AFRICOM the opportunity to address defense-related concerns in an unprecedented fashion. For example, our efforts to streamline communication and integrate a whole-of-government approach to U.S. posture in Africa allowed us to effectively deliver International Military Education and Training (IMET) programs, sponsored by the Department of State, to our African partners. Near the end of my command in 2010, approximately 900 military and civilian students from 44 African countries received education and training through the IMET program in the United States; many of these graduates filled key positions in their respective militaries and governments. The enduring relationships fostered through IMET deepen U.S. partnership with these nations and fosters the promotion of an active civil society in developing nations.

AFRICOM works closely with USAID as well. Like the U.S. military, USAID is action oriented through its programs, delivering aid and developmental enhancements in African nations for various crises such as Ebola and drought relief, and implementing life-saving programs like PEPFAR. Given its structure and the long-term development goals it works toward, USAID is well situated to continue delivering such health, educational and societal assistance as an autonomous agency, rather than as an entity directly folded into the State Department.

USAID's frontline work in Africa is essential to ensuring successful implementation of U.S. foreign policy throughout the continent. This past April, USAID announced it provided humanitarian assistance to over two million Zimbabweans following wide spread crop failure brought about by recent droughts. In November 2016, USAID deployed a disaster assistance response team to Nigeria to help support Nigeria's efforts in reducing food insecurity caused by Boko Haram. These are only a few initiatives USAID is leading in Africa; the Department of State simply does not have the capacity to carry out these programs and if USAID was not present in Africa, it would fall to the military to fulfill these initiatives.

U.S. Air Forces Africa (AFAFRICA), along with the component commands of AFRICOM, achieved full operational capability during my tenure as AFRICOM Commander and played an instrumental role in supporting humanitarian operations. However, to be responsible for administering all USAID-like programs would be far outside the scope and function of the U.S. military. As I said during my confirmation hearing to be commander of AFRICOM, "The U.S. military is not an instrument of first resort in providing humanitarian assistance but supports civilian relief agencies." In my estimation, the roles and responsibilities of the Department of State, USAID, and AFRICOM, as currently constructed, serve our interests in Africa very well, when adequately resourced. Altering these arrangements would lead to confusion among our partners, would have a negative impact on regional security affairs and undermine efforts to advance U.S. national security interests.

I have seen firsthand the importance of how development assistance can transform communities. While conducting military exercises with African partners in Senegal, exercise related construction was required through a local community to transport our forces to the location of a joint exercise. Instead of building a road only to serve the military forces, we spoke with local community leaders to identify where the road could also best meet the needs of the community, post exercise. Because of our collaboration, the road connected neighboring towns, providing avenues for greater economic development and government access.

Likewise, on the island of Comoros, USAID was working to support the health and educational needs of a community, but needed a durable facility and clean water to help implement the program. USAID does not have the capacity to build their own facilities. But with our construction engineers needing to maintain mission related expeditionary skills, we put the Seabees to work for them to build the facility and Army engineers to drill the important well. The facilityl, which accommodates about 250 students who attend the U.S. equivalent of high school and junior college on the island of Grande Comore, was the third such project the U.S. military built there since 2007 when they were deployed in the region. I had the opportunity to tour the site and told them with pride, "You're here to help in an area that makes the greatest difference for the children."

These are just a few examples of how creating strong foundations for our African partners helps to achieve sustained development. These investments must be continued; the cost of the investment is small when compared to the positive economic returns and investments in stability enjoyed by host nations. The more comprehensive engagement there is from the United States, the more stable these partner countries become. And that has a clear strategic benefit to the United States.

Thank you for inviting me to testify before the Committee today. I look forward to answering any questions you may have.

———

Chairman ROYCE. Thank you, General Ward. Thank you very much for agreeing to testify here today. We are going to go to Mr. Bryan Christy, but I understand that Mr. Christy has a 1-minute video that he would like us to contemplate here.

STATEMENT OF MR. BRYAN CHRISTY, EXPLORER AND INVESTIGATIVE REPORTER, NATIONAL GEOGRAPHIC SOCIETY

Mr. CHRISTY. Yes, sir. We are National Geographic so we come with our toys.

[Video shown.]

Mr. CHRISTY. Chairman Royce.

Chairman ROYCE. Mr. Christy, you have our attention.

Mr. CHRISTY. I can never live up to the technics of National Geographic film crews.

Chairman Royce, Ranking Member Engel, distinguished members of the committee, I would like to thank you for holding this important hearing today to explore ways to strengthen U.S. ties with African countries. The leadership of this committee on enhancing this bond is critical and I am grateful for the opportunity to share my expertise to assist with your mission.

My name is Bryan Christy. I am a journalist with National Geographic Society Explorer. My specialty is international wildlife crime. For the past 7 years I have focused almost exclusively on investigating the killing of elephants and rhinos for their ivory and horns. I do not come to this field as a biologist specializing in animals, I come to it as a lawyer turned investigator specializing in transnational crimes with strategic significance.

Illegal wildlife trade amounts to billions of dollars per year inspiring corruption, murder, the destabilization of governments, the spread of disease, the devastation of species, and the destruction of ecosystems. The negative impact of the ivory and rhino horn trade is so great it warrants classifying elephants and rhinos as global strategic resources.

This morning, however, I would like to draw the committee's attention to the people on the ground who protect wildlife in protected areas—park rangers, game wardens, and other local crime fighters—who find themselves in a battle that extends well beyond wildlife, a battle against transnational criminal enterprises including terrorist and extremist groups which underscores America's interest in Africa and its wildlife.

Many of the most violent terrorist and extremist groups operating in Africa today have sought or currently find refuge in parks or protected areas—Boko Haram in Sambisa Forest, Nigeria; Joseph Kony and his Lord's Resistance Army in Garamba National Park in the Democratic Republic of Congo; the FDLR; the Rwandan Hutu rebel militia in Virunga National Park, DRC, the perpetrators of the '94 Rwandan genocide in which 800,000 people died. This list goes on.

Many of these groups traffic ivory or rhino horn for arms and other needs including the LRA, the FDLR, Seleka, and al-Qaeda linked groups operating in Mali where three al-Qaeda linked Islamic extremist groups have recently merged. Other groups such as Al Shabaab in Somalia and FDLR in the Congo exploit forest resources to finance themselves, taxing charcoal for example. These groups are responsible for massive destabilization across the continent. Boko Haram has been implicated in the murder of 15,000 people and the displacement of more than 2 million. Kony's LRA has abducted over 7,000 people and killed more than 3,000 others.

Park rangers are often their victims. In 2014, Virunga's chief ranger Emmanuel de Merode was shot four times in the stomach and legs. This extraordinary champion for economic development and conservation in the Congo continues his work running the most dangerous park in the world to be a park ranger where he has lost more than 40 men under his command.

Two weeks ago, a section of his park was overrun by about 300 suspected ADF, Ugandan jihadist militia, and Mai-Mai militia. Losses have been reported on both sides and they engaged again on Monday. These groups are using forests as hideouts and to exploit villages for their food, shelter, water, and medicines. They rape, murder, they kidnap children, they compromise the security of forests where doctors and researchers might investigate emerging disease such as Ebola and the Marburg virus.

In this environment, park rangers operate as a first line of defense not just for animals but also for people. In many cases, park rangers are the only legitimate law enforcement to protect and stabilize these communities, and what happens to communities in this part of the world all too often happens for these countries as well. This is not a call for indiscriminate militarization. When soldiers bring weapons into the bush they tend to use them, decimating species and exacerbating wildlife and resource trafficking.

But by addressing the needs of park rangers and other stewards on the ground in Africa, by facilitating networking among rangers around the world, by training prosecutors and judges regarding wildlife crime, by supporting a free press, by working to reduce demand for threatened wildlife, and by engaging at a diplomatic level with government leaders across the continent regarding wildlife crime and violent extremism, the United States has an opportunity to advance its interests in national security, health, human rights, the environment, and wildlife.

I would again like to thank Chairman Royce, Ranking Member Engel, and the full committee for allowing me to submit testimony today. Your legislation, the END Wildlife Trafficking Act signed into law in 2016, is exactly the kind of leadership the world needs. I look forward to working further to advance these goals and am happy to take your questions.

[The prepared statement of Mr. Christy follows:]

Testimony of Bryan Christy

Explorer Program Fellow, Special Investigations, National Geographic Society

Committee on Foreign Affairs, U.S. House of Representatives

"U.S. Interests in Africa"

18 May 2017

Chairman Royce, Ranking Member Engel, and distinguished members of the Committee, I would like to thank you for holding this important hearing today to explore methods for strengthening U.S. ties with African countries. The leadership of the Committee on enhancing this bond is critical, and I am grateful for the opportunity to share my expertise and assist with your mission.

Park rangers, game wardens, and other wildlife crime fighters operating in Africa represent order in rural and wild places under siege by terrorist and other criminal enterprises, transforming these traditional protectors of wildlife and protected areas into a first line of defense against terrorism, destabilized states, emerging disease, human rights abuses, and corruption.

The United States has a direct interest in staunching terrorism and other transnational crimes, in reducing global instability, in anticipating emerging diseases such as Ebola, and in conserving the world's most valued wildlife and natural resources for the health of global ecosystems and the enjoyment of current and future generations.

The United States has elevated its focus on wildlife trafficking through such official measures as President Obama's Executive Order "Combatting Wildlife Trafficking," which established a cabinet-level wildlife trafficking taskforce,[i] and President Trump's Executive Order, "Enforcing Federal Law with Respect to Transnational Criminal Organizations and Preventing International Trafficking."[ii] Congress's recent bipartisan passage of the Eliminate, Neutralize, and Disrupt (END) Wildlife Trafficking Act signed into law in 2016 further clarifies U.S. interests in wildlife trafficking and sets priorities for addressing it.

My testimony this morning will address organized crime, extremist militias, and terrorism as they relate to Africa's wildlife, protected areas, and park rangers. I note that journalists across Africa risk violence, incarceration, and worse for reporting on crime involving the powerful or corrupt, including on wildlife crime. It is therefore from a privileged position that a foreign journalist like myself comments on crime in Africa. Issues of poverty, climate change-induced drought, population growth, and other worthy and pressing concerns for Africa and U.S. interests are outside the scope of my testimony.

ORGANIZED CRIME

Transnational wildlife crime represents a transfer of life from range states, primarily in Africa, Southeast Asia, and South America to its consumers, typically in north Asia, Europe, and the United States. Organized criminal syndicates traffic nearly every part of most of the threated or endangered animals on the planet, including elephant teeth, rhinoceros horn, shark fins, tiger pelts, bear paws, pangolin scales, and more. They move live animals including apes, monkeys, big cats, rare birds, and reptiles. They

destroy entire ecosystems, plundering forests of protected timber to supply the furniture industry, vacuuming coral reefs and their inhabitants to supply the aquarium trade.

An estimated 30,000 African elephants are illegally killed each year for their teeth, an unsustainable rate which unchecked will lead to the animals' extinction. Rhinos face similar pressures for their horns, and already several rhinoceros species are recently extinct in Africa and Asia.

The wildlife trafficking problem is widely known, though not adequately addressed in many African countries even in terms of basic, intelligence-led investigative techniques, prosecutions, and convictions. Rarely is a trafficking kingpin identified, let alone brought to justice.

Corruption remains a significant problem in many range and consumer states. Ivory and rhino horn-related corruption infects park rangers, police, customs officers, prosecutors, judges, and politicians. It pits law enforcement against itself. In South Africa's Kruger National Park, for example, home to the world's largest wild rhinoceros population, park rangers cannot take poaching cases to local police or judges due to corruption.

Many countries fail to recognize the significance of wildlife crime in terms of economic value to criminals and cost to ecosystems. This failure to adequately prioritize wildlife crime and to enforce wildlife laws is what makes it so highly lucrative to transnational criminal syndicates. In some cases laws are inadequate to the crimes, in others, laws may carry penalties judges consider too severe to impose on a wildlife trafficker.

Finding a balance between crimes and penalties, educating prosecutors and judges, and supporting well-functioning judicial systems are in the interest of the United States.

TERRORISM

Park rangers, game wardens, and other wildlife crime fighters in Africa represent a front line against terrorism, extremist groups, and violent militias.[iii] Park rangers protect wildlife and wild spaces, but they also represent a local police force, often the only trustworthy police force in remote areas, making them important to the stability of communities throughout the continent, and of value to advancing U.S. interests in stabilized states, the study and management of emerging diseases, the protection of human rights, and the prosecution of wildlife criminals.

Terrorists Hide In Parks

Many of the most dangerous extremist and militia groups operating in Africa today have sought or currently find refuge inside forests and protected areas. These include Boko Haram in Sambisa Forest[iv], Nigeria; Joseph Kony and his Lord's Resistance Army in Garamba National Park, Democratic Republic of Congo (DRC); and the FDLR, the Rwandan Hutu rebel militia in Virunga National Park, DRC, perpetrators of the 1994 Rwandan genocide in which 800,000 people died.

Other extremist groups, such as Al Shabaab in Somalia exploit forest resources to finance themselves, taxing charcoal, for example, in the case of Shabaab; or killing elephants for ivory in the case of Seleka, an alliance of mostly Muslim rebel groups whose battle with the Christian and animist rebel group, Anti-Balaka, have thrust the Central African Republic into civil war.

NATIONAL GEOGRAPHIC

Elephants and Rhinos as Strategic Resources

Ivory and rhino horn are trafficked for cash by criminal organizations in Africa, Asia, and the West and used as currency by terrorist groups to buy arms, medicine, and other necessities, transforming these animals and their parts into strategic resources for criminal and terrorist organizations.

South Sudan. The Central African Republic (CAR). The DRC. Sudan. Chad. Five of the world's least stable nations, as ranked by the Washington, D.C.-based organization the Fund for Peace, are home to groups who travel to other countries to kill elephants.

The Lord's Resistance Army, Seleka, the FDLR, and extremist groups operating in Mali, where rangers are regularly a target of "terrorist armed groups,"[v] have been implicated in ivory trafficking, as well.

Wildlife trafficking is a destabilizing force in even established African countries such as Kenya, Tanzania and South Africa. Each has faced significant corruption, sometimes at even the highest levels of government, involving illegal trade in elephant ivory and rhino horn. Protecting these strategic species and reducing demand for their parts in Asia and the rest of the world cuts off funds to transnational criminals, including violent militias and terrorists.

Sudan: A Poaching Super State

Combining both criminality and support for violent groups, Sudan bears attention. Though it has no elephants of its own, Sudan is both home and host to elephant poachers and ivory traffickers--including the Janjaweed, the Lord's Resistance Army, and Sudanese Armed Forces--who use the country, especially Darfur, as home base, and travel across the continent to kill elephants in national parks and protected areas.

Sudan's president Omar al-Bashir, who has been indicted by the International Criminal Court for war crimes and crimes against humanity for actions in Darfur, protects these groups which engage in elephant killing raids on foot and on horseback. Raids launched from Sudan and Chad have resulted in some of the most brutal elephant killings in modern history, including the killing of as many as 650 elephants in Cameroon in 2012.

Elephant poaching by those sequestered in and around Sudan is not as high as that in East and lately southern Africa in terms of number of elephants killed, but it is more violent, more disruptive to society, and it is resulting in murdered rangers across the region, including in Garamba National Park and Zakouma National Park in Chad.

Terrorist and Rebel Groups are Connecting

In some cases, Africa's most violent groups are connecting with each other, and seek relations outside the continent. Boko Haram leader Abubakar Shekau pledged allegiance to ISIS in 2015,[vi] leading to Boko Haram's being designated the terrorist group's West African province (ISWAP), a relationship continued by Shekau's faction, and by that of a second Boko Haram faction leader, Abu Musab al-Barnawi, according to reports citing the ISIS-linked magazine, *Al-Naba*.[vii]

Joseph Kony's LRA has linked with Seleka in the CAR, and Kony expressed an intention to establish relations with Boko Haram, according to an LRA defector I interviewed in 2014.[viii]

Al Shabaab represents the Somali affiliate of Al-Qaeda.

In Mali, where Al-Qaeda in the Islamic Maghreb (AQIM) continues to expand,[ix] taking on new partners earlier this year,[x] extremist groups have been linked to elephant poaching and the killing of wildlife rangers.[xi]

Beyond Wildlife: Extraordinary Costs to Human Life and State Stability

Taken together, these terrorist and militia groups represent a staggering impact on people, wildlife, and governance across Africa. Often the only legitimate force in place in remote and rural areas to oppose these groups are park rangers and game wardens.

Hundreds of FDLR currently occupy Virunga National Park, making it the most dangerous park in the world to be a park ranger. In 2014, Virunga's Chief Ranger, Emmanuel de Merode was shot four times in the stomach and legs by unidentified assailants at a time when his park was under pressure from illegal fishing operators on Lake Edward, charcoal traffickers, elephant poachers, and international oil interests seeking to open up the park. Considered a hero by his fellow rangers, de Merode has sought to bring sustainable development to the park while at the same time routing corruption, and protecting the park and its wildlife. De Merode, whose rangers protect the world's largest remaining population of mountain gorillas, has lost 41 men under his command and his park has lost at least 150 rangers since civil war began in the DRC.

During a series of raids beginning in December 2008, Joseph Kony's LRA killed 800 people, including 8 Garamba rangers and staff, kidnapped 160 children, and displaced 100,000 people. Since it began recording data in 2008, the group Invisible Children has recorded 2,339 LRA attacks on civilians in which they abducted 7,565 people and killed 3,116 others in CAR, DRC, and South Sudan.

Boko Haram, kidnapper of school children, has been implicated in the deaths of 15,000 people and the displacement of more than 2 million.

These groups often do not occupy parks solely, or even primarily, for their wildlife. They occupy them as hideouts and as places from which to prey on villagers for food, water and medicine. Their crimes include murder, rape and kidnapping. They poach animals for food, to traffic their parts as bushmeat, and to exchange for weapons and other needs.

They also kill wildlife to send a message to wildlife rangers and others who might oppose them. In Virunga, charcoal traffickers killed six mountain gorillas in 2012 in an effort to eliminate what they perceived to be a main driver of public opposition to their illegal trade, gorilla-related tourism.

Rangers Represent Order and are Being Killed for It

Park rangers do more than protect wildlife. They secure land, protect villagers, and help stabilize communities. In many places, police and military are corrupt. To see a police officer, soldier, or even a United Nations peacekeeping representative at your doorstep can be to fear for your property, your safety, even your life. The 2015 alleged rape of citizens by U.N. MINUSCA peacekeepers operating in CAR underscores that security in central Africa is a rare and precious resource.

In remote and rural areas park rangers and game wardens are often the only law enforcement standing between violent groups and the villagers on whom they prey. As a result, these groups target park rangers not for animals, but to advance their lawlessness. Protected areas in Central Africa and West Africa can represent islands of stability in oceans of chaos.

Rangers' protection of land and community creates an opportunity to replenish wildlife destroyed by poaching. But once the land is lost, that opportunity is gone. Supporting rangers secures habitat as a hedge against extinction.

Garamba: A Killing Zone

Rangers on the ground are often insufficiently equipped to take on the militarized, mechanized, organized force they must confront. In Garamba National Park, for example, there are signs elephants having been shot through the tops of their heads from helicopters. Yet I witnessed rangers having to work with limited ammunition and to use compromised weapons taken from poachers because of red tape involved in legally acquiring adequate weapons.

Villagers along the park's perimeter told me they considered Garamba's park rangers to be their most important protectors. The park is managed by the non-governmental organization, African Parks Congo, an affiliate of African Parks of South Africa, in partnership with the Congolese Institute for Nature Conservation (ICCN). In Garamba, as with many other key parks, rangers build schools, medical facilities, churches and mosques. Importantly, when the LRA and other groups attack the park they do it not only to raid the park's ivory stockpile, they do it to kill the rangers who stand between the terrorists and the people they want to murder, rape, and kidnap, and for the food and medicine they want to steal. Rangers represent order and they're being killed for it.

In the past ten years, Garamba has lost 22 rangers; two were killed last month.

Bushmeat and Emerging Disease

Stability is an underappreciated element in controlling the emergence and spread of disease. The Ebola epidemic in West Africa, 2014-2015, was made vastly worse by 20 years of political upheaval and civil wars in Guinea, Liberia, and Sierra Leone, which had so weakened their infrastructures generally and health care systems in particular that the outbreak was made much worse. Every Ebola outbreak since the first known appearance of the disease, in 1976, killed only two or three hundred people at most— whereas this event in West Africa killed more than 11,000, sickened more than 27,000, and cost billions of dollars, including millions to the US. The Ebola virus itself was not different from earlier outbreaks. The circumstances of those societies were different, and as a result, an outbreak became an epidemic, spreading costs and fear around the world.

By providing stability in remote areas, rangers play an important prophylactic role against disease. The community liaison work of rangers on the ground open doors when diseases emerge. Rangers facilitate intelligence gathering across the continent, offering ways of sharing international values with isolated communities.

The benefits of support for park rangers and other wildlife crime fighters includes disrupting trade in animal species (bushmeat trade) that carry, or can cause, deadly disease in humans, as well as in providing security in remote areas where study or treatment of emerging diseases is important.

All over Central Africa the direct hunting of, and trade in, bushmeat of certain types exposes people to extreme jeopardy of Ebola and Marburg virus. The species include gorillas, chimps, and (for Marburg, and possibly also Ebola) giant fruit bats, which are also harvested in great numbers as food.

Rangers police the bushmeat trade, and represent potential security for doctors and medical researchers investigating emerging diseases in remote areas.

OPPORTUNITIES

Diplomacy and Demand Reduction

Diplomacy was critical to an historic agreement between President Xi of China and President Obama to eliminate their country's respective ivory industries. Demand for wildlife products in Asia, especially ivory and rhino horn, is a driver of international crime, including terrorism, in Africa. China has since promised to shutdown its ivory industry by the end of this year.[xii]

Further efforts to reduce demand in China, as well as in likely spillover countries in Southeast Asia, including Cambodia, Laos, Myanmar, Thailand and Vietnam, are necessary to give effect to the commitments by China and the U.S., and to anticipate increased trafficking to those countries as their economies grow.

Information Sharing

Free Press is Critical

In most African countries, if not all, journalists struggle to investigate and report stories involving political corruption. In some cases the media is state controlled. In others it's owned by conglomerates involved in corruption. More than once I've asked an African journalist why he or she doesn't report a story I would want to report on if it were happening in my country. The answer I get is, "I would be killed if I wrote that story." This needs to change.

Empower Individuals

In 2013, the State Department invited me to West Africa as part of its Speakers Program to give a series of talks to government officials there about ivory trafficking. Togo has almost no elephants, but it was in the process of completing the second largest deep water port in Sub-Saharan Africa. I suggested Togo would likely see an effort by international traffickers to smuggle ivory through their new port. Sitting in the audience that day was a young officer from Togo's Office Against Narcotics and Money Laundering, Lieutenant Essossimna Awi. Awi returned to the port where he took one of the scanners his team was using to x-ray incoming shipping containers for drugs and weapons, and turned it around to x-ray, for the first time, outgoing shipments. A few months later he made the largest ivory seizure in African history, over 4 tons hidden inside a shipment of timber bound for Vietnam. Secretary of State John Kerry personally telephoned President Faure to commend his country's success. Faure then published an op-ed challenging other countries to join his country's fight,[xiii] was given a seat on Interpol's program focused on wildlife crime, and emerged as a leader on the issue.

Important U.S. Programs

The United States has much to offer Africa in terms of training, resources, and diplomacy. Programs that bring together law enforcement, judiciary, journalists, and others, separately or together, to enable

them to network are invaluable to countering transnational criminal syndicates that do not face diplomatic limitations on crossing borders.

I do not pretend to have comprehensive knowledge of programs that might advance the interests I've raised this morning. I can cite some programs I've encountered that seem to be on the right track, in addition to the efforts by the many conservation organizations whose work is important, but which are too numerous to mention.

Programs with important impact that seek to improve enforcement across Africa include the International Attaché program operated by the U.S. Fish & Wildlife Service Office of Law Enforcement, the State Department's Speaker's Program and its International Visitor Leadership Program, the EAGLE Network's non-governmental effort to monitor and support prosecutions, and various Wildlife Enforcement Networks (WENs).

Access to equipment and materiel requires both funding and government authorization. The problem is not always a matter of ability to pay for munitions, but rather the ability to access materiel in countries where government or military leadership restricts importation or carrying of arms out of fear those weapons may be turned against the state. Here U.S. diplomacy might help.

In 2016, National Geographic hosted an evening to bring together Africa's park rangers as part of the U.S. Fish and Wildlife Service's International Conservation Chiefs Academy.[xiv] Criminals, including terrorists, operate across national lines, but law enforcement often lacks the funding, authority, or relationships to do the same. A similar program, National Association of Conservation Law Enforcement Chiefs (NACLEC) is run for domestic enforcement chiefs in the U.S. Building personal and institutional relationships among officers and government officials is one way to bridge this gap.

A number of U.S. programs directed at protecting key species, land, and community have had important impacts for elephants, rhinoceroses, big cats, great apes, and marine turtles as part of the so-called Multinational Species Conservation Acts enacted by Congress.[xv] The Eliminate, Neutralize, and Disrupt (END) Wildlife Trafficking Act signed into law in 2016 likewise makes an important contribution to tackling transnational wildlife crime, and I look forward to its impact.

Conclusion

By focusing on the needs of park rangers and other stewards on the ground in Africa, by encouraging networking among rangers around the world, by training prosecutors and judges regarding wildlife crime, by supporting a free press, by working to reduce demand, and by engaging at a diplomatic level with government leaders across the continent regarding wildlife crime and violent extremism, the U.S. has an opportunity to advance its interests in national security, health, human rights, the environment, and wildlife.

In conclusion, Congress has the ability to advance positive policies that would enhance the relationship between the United States and countries throughout Africa. I would again like to thank Chairman Royce, Ranking Member Engel, and the full committee for allowing me to submit testimony today. I look forward to working further to advance these goals.

i https://obamawhitehouse.archives.gov/the-press-office/2013/07/01/executive-order-combating-wildlife-trafficking

ii https://www.whitehouse.gov/the-press-office/2017/02/09/presidential-executive-order-enforcing-federal-law-respect-transnational

iii http://www.nationalgeographic.com/tracking-ivory/article.html

iv http://www.aljazeera.com/news/2016/12/buhari-boko-haram-base-retaken-sambisa-forest-161224125809113.html

v https://minusma.unmissions.org/point-de-presse-jeudi-8-octobre-2015

vi http://www.nationalgeographic.com/tracking-ivory/article.html

vii http://www.newsweek.com/boko-haram-isis-abubakar-shekau-abu-musab-al-barnawi-496615

viii http://www.nationalgeographic.com/tracking-ivory/article.html

ix https://www.nytimes.com/2016/03/16/world/africa/al-qaedas-african-offshoot-makes-a-lethal-comeback.html?_r=1

x http://www.news24.com/Africa/News/3-islamic-extremist-groups-in-mali-merge-pledge-to-al-qaeda-20170303

xi https://minusma.unmissions.org/point-de-presse-jeudi-8-octobre-2015; http://www.foxnews.com/world/2017/03/02/3-mali-islamic-extremist-groups-merge-pledge-to-al-qaida.html; http://www.rfi.fr/afrique/20151018-mali-elephants-morts-braconnage-groupes-terroristes

xii http://news.nationalgeographic.com/2016/12/wildlife-watch-china-legal-ivory-market-african-elephants/

xiii https://www.independent.co.uk/voices/comment/faure-gnassingb-failure-to-act-on-poaching-will-place-elephants-on-the-path-to-extinction-9121960.html

xiv https://www.fws.gov/le/lcca/index.html

xv https://www.fws.gov/international/laws-treaties-agreements/us-conservation-laws/multinational-species-conservation-acts.html

Chairman ROYCE. Well, thank you, Mr. Christy. We go now to Mr. Carroll.

STATEMENT OF MR. ANTHONY CARROLL, ADJUNCT PROFESSOR, SCHOOL OF ADVANCED INTERNATIONAL STUDIES, JOHNS HOPKINS UNIVERSITY

Mr. CARROLL. Thank you, Mr. Chairman. This month marks the 17th anniversary of the signing into law of AGOA. That historic legislation would not have been enacted without the efforts of yourself and other members in this room, along with those members no longer in Congress including Jim McDermott, Phil Crane, Charlie Rangel, Bill Thomas, Don Payne, and Bill Archer.

Since AGOA's passage, the economic landscape in Africa has changed dramatically. First, as you noted in your introductory remarks, between 2008 and '14 Africa's GDP grew an average of 5 percent, with some countries exceeding 8 percent annual GDP growth. The most dynamic growth is Africa's burgeoning services sector. Second, overseas development assistance, including from the U.S., has fallen behind foreign direct investment and remittances and volume of financial flows into Africa. And last, as you noted earlier, China is now Africa's largest trading partner at $172 billion in annual trade last year, twice that of the United States, and Africa's investment patterns have followed suit.

I will devote my testimony to the examination of the relationship between trade investment and identify the ways in which the U.S. and Africa can benefit from an expanding relationship. AGOA has produced a modicum of success. Two-way trade between Africa and the United States is approximately $80 billion a year. From 2000 to 2016, non-petroleum imports from AGOA countries have shown strong growth of 75 percent over the same period, mostly concentrated in automobiles, apparel, and agricultural products.

China's trade has been criticized as being unbalanced and defined by the export of raw commodities from Africa and the import of finished goods from China to Africa. In contrast, AGOA trade includes sophisticated products such as luxury automobiles and fine wine from South Africa; fashion apparel from Lesotho, Mauritius, and Kenya; cut flowers from Kenya and Ethiopia; and gem diamonds from Botswana and Namibia. Some of those aren't captured in trade data as they are sent through third countries. Indeed, the United States purchases over one-third of Africa's diamonds.

At the same time, U.S. trade balances with AGOA countries has improved significantly since 2000. Focusing on non-petroleum trade, U.S. trade balances improved from a 1.3 billion trade deficit in 2000 to an 831 million trade surplus in 2016. U.S. exports to the AGOA countries have grown by a greater percentage since 2000, up 130 percent, than have U.S. imports from the same countries, up 75 percent. This is a winning program for U.S. jobs.

Although job creation statistics in Africa are at best estimates, it is widely believed that AGOA has created hundreds of thousands of new direct and indirect jobs in Africa and the United States. In South Africa alone, it is estimated that 60,000 direct jobs have been created by AGOA and another 100,000 indirect. In investment, the U.S. remains a major investor in Africa. Blue Chip companies not only bring, U.S. companies bring money, but they also bring best operating global practices, technology, and training. In 2016, the U.S. invested just under $4 billion in Africa.

Indeed, there is a relationship between investment and trade. For example, GE invested in a locomotive manufacturing plant in South Africa in accordance with local content, and most of those imports are coming from the United States. The China experience has been noted before. Clearly, China's growth not only in trade but in investment has grown to $60 billion, $36 billion last year, and with the FOCAC and One Belt, One Road conferences recently being convened that is going to expand dramatically.

Trade capacity development has been a partner to U.S. increased AGOA imports. The U.S. development agencies have spent nearly $500 million in trade capacity development, and this trade has been run through the various trade hubs in Africa. These trade hubs have supported $854 million in African exports to the United States and elsewhere and $195 million in leveraged investments. Because of the interest among Africans to increase U.S. investment into Africa and not just development assistance, these Hubs have broadened their mandate to include new capabilities in fostering links between U.S. investors and African opportunities at the firm, project, and sectoral level. Just this month, USAID led a group of pension investors to Africa and will organize a reverse mission later in the year.

Africa is the population center of the world in the next two generations. And while that presents an opportunity in providing labor surplus and opportunities for manufacturing, it is also a challenge because if not harnessed well it could create the opportunities for terrorism and massive immigration as we have seen.

So some of the recommendations that I have in terms of expanding U.S. investment relations with Africa are continued efforts to increase market size. Many American companies eschew opportunities in investing in Africa because African markets are relatively small at the national level.

We should continue our efforts to expand African regional integration. Enhance U.S. investment in infrastructure. The Millennium Challenge Corporation has created a new model that requires greater accountability and partnership with our African partner countries. However, one of the absences in MCC is the growth of subnational debt instruments. I believe MCC should devote—as I recommended 4 years ago—in terms of regional funds MCC should consider expending a portion of their funds to subnational infrastructure projects, because I believe that is often the greater and stronger relationship to build infrastructure.

We need to continue to strengthen Africa's innovation in enabling business environments. That includes measures such as IPR protection, but also tax and financial incentives to really give Africa's innovation communities the opportunity to grow. I believe that the U.S. in sharing at almost a firm level fostering exchanges such as the Global Entrepreneurship Forum, AGOA Forum, and others are an opportunity for us to expand at a firm to firm and innovator to innovator way and opportunity for U.S. investment to flow.

Let me close by saying that—and Congressman Yoho was going to testify or present at the Center for Global Development the other day, so I thought it was appropriate for me to mention that

I believe that the instrumentalities and instruments provided by OPIC, EXIM, and TDA are important to continue and deepen our trade and investment relationships with Africa. Much to the contrary I believe OPIC is a fundamental tool to really engender and gain the interest of small and medium enterprises of the United States, whereas because only 8 percent of its services are used by Fortune 500 companies I believe that OPIC and EXIM can provide a platform to improve and increase our trade investment.

And lastly, I think it would be remiss for me not to mention the important work of the U.S. Foreign Commercial Service, the Foreign Agricultural Service, and domestic U.S. Department of Commerce offices to not only broadcast but even inform business communities about the myriad opportunities of trade and investment in Africa. Thank you very much, Mr. Chairman.

[The prepared statement of Mr. Carroll follows:]

Testimony
House Foreign Affairs Committee
May 17, 2017

Anthony Carroll
Adjunct Professor
John Hopkins University
School of Advanced International Studies*

This month marks the seventeenth anniversary of the signing into law of the Africa Growth and Opportunity Act (AGOA). That historic legislation would not have been enacted without the efforts of Chairman Ed Royce and a bipartisan group of Congressmen and Congresswomen who wanted to create a new economic relationship with Africa. I specially note the contributions of Jim McDermott, Phil Crane, Charlie Rangel, Bill Thomas, Don Payne and Bill Archer. Since AGOA's passage Africa's economic landscape has changed dramatically. First, from 2008-2014, Africa's GDP grew on average 5% per annum with some Africa countries achieving above 8% annual GDP growth. And the most dynamic element of this growth has been Africa's burgeoning services sector. Second, Overseas Development Assistant (ODA) has fallen behind foreign direct investment (FDI) and remittances in volume of financial flows to Africa. And last, in 2009, China became Africa's largest trading partner with last year's total trade at $172 billion, over twice that of the U.S. China's investment patterns have followed suit.

I will devote my testimony to an examination of the relationship between trade and investment and will identify ways in which both the United States and Africa can benefit from an expanding relationship. My observations are based upon nearly 40 years of advising companies, development agencies, foundations and regional and international organizations on African trade, development and investment and as a private equity investor in various sectors. I will also look at the various tools that the U.S. can utilize to deepen that relationship and contrast the roles China and South Africa.

Trade

AGOA has produced a modicum of success. Total two-way trade (AGOA and non-AGOA) between Africa and the US is approximately $80 billion per year. if you disregard oil imports, which skew assessments of AGOA's impact because (1) oil imports really have not been created by or even much affected by AGOA, and (2) commodity price fluctuations can have a profound impact on trade statistics without reflecting fundamental changes.

According to USITC's Dataweb, while petroleum imports from the AGOA countries have fallen rather sharply from 2000 to 2016 (-66% by volume, -47% by value), non-petroleum imports from the AGOA countries have shown strong growth up 75% over the same period from $6.9 billion in 2000 to $12.2 billion in 2016. This growth has been concentrated mainly in automobiles, apparel and agricultural products. China's trade has been criticized as being unbalanced and defined by the export of raw commodities from Africa and the export of consumer goods from China to Africa. In contrast, AGOA trade includes sophisticated products such as luxury automobiles and fine wine from South Africa and fashion apparel from Lesotho, Mauritius and Kenya. Some trade such as cut flowers from Kenya and Ethiopia and gem diamonds from Botswana and Namibia are not captured by AGOA trade data as they sent through third countries. Indeed, the US purchases over 1/3 of Africa's diamonds.

At the same time, the US trade balance with the AGOA countries has improved significantly since 2000. Focusing on non-petroleum trade, the US trade balance has improved from a $1.3 billion trade deficit in 2000 to an $831 billion trade surplus in 2016. (If you include petroleum (which is a mistake in my opinion), the U.S. trade balance has improved significantly but remains in deficit, improving from -$16.0 billion in 2000 to -$7.0 billion in 2016.) US exports to the AGOA countries have grown by a greater percentage since 2000 (up 130%) than have US imports from the same countries (up 75%). This is a winning program for U.S. jobs!

Much is made by the critics of AGOA of the supposed fact that the benefits are highly concentrated in just a few countries, but this is not correct.. 36 of the 38 eligible AGOA beneficiaries have regularly exported to the US under AGOA, although in many instances the volumes are quite small. Although job creation statistics in Africa are at best estimates, it is widely believed that AGOA has created hundreds of thousands of new direct jobs and millions of indirect jobs in Africa AND in the United States. In South Africa, it is estimated that 60,000 direct jobs have been created by AGOA and another 100,000 indirect jobs.

In short, I believe there is a very positive story to tell about AGOA, and hopefully the 10-year extension of AGOA in 2015 will provide further impetus for even more growth.

US Investment

The US remains a major foreign investor into Africa. "Blue Chip" US companies like GE, Cargill, Johnson & Johnson, Newmont, Merck, Exxon Mobil and Anadarko not only bring money but also global best operating practices, technology and training to Africa. According to the latest UNCTAD data, in 2015 the US was Africa's largest cumulative non-Asian foreign investor at $66 billion followed closely by the UK and France. In 2016, the US invested just under $4 billion in Africa. Indeed, there is a relationship with U.S. investment and trade. For example, GE invested in a locomotive manufacturing plant in SA in accordance with local content rules. However, 50% of the content is from US suppliers.

China Investment

According to my SAIS colleagues at the China Africa Research Initiative, China's FDI between 2000-2014 was $86 billion. Just between 2014-2016 China quadrupled its investment into Africa to $36 billion last year. The growth of Chinese investment into Africa has continued to expand In a recent Business Daily (Kenya) article, China is reporting a 64% increase in Africa FDI during the first quarter of 2017. Unlike US FDI which is largely private sector led, Chinese investment is a blend of state and non-state actors and often in the form of long term loans and is often geared toward infrastructure development such as the railroads and hydroelectric power dams. However, the recent growth of Chinese FDI into Ethiopia's manufacturing sector by private companies is perhaps evidence of changing trend. At last year's Forum on China Africa Cooperation (FOCAC), China committed $60 billion in infrastructure investment in Africa over the next five years. This month's One Belt on Road meeting in China is evidence of China's long term commitment to infrastructure across the globe to foster increased trade and Africa is a major target of the initiative. While the numbers are hard to quantify because of the interfirm nature of transactions, South Africa has also become a larger investor into Africa than the US and its brands (Shoprite, Standard Bank, Castle) evident everywhere.

Trade Capacity Development

In truth, AGOA is as much as a development as it is trade initiative. Since inception, the U.S. has spent nearly $500 million on trade capacity assistance in Africa. But this assistance has also been coupled with country led measures that may not have been instituted without AGOA's compliance incentives. The chief vehicle for trade capacity assistance has been USAID's three regional Trade Hubs. These Hubs have been effective in improving the enabling environment for trade on the national and regional level as well as enhancing the capacity of African firms to access the US and global markets. Since their inception in the early 2000s, the Trade Hubs have supported $854 million in African exports and $195 million in leveraged investments. Because of the interest among Africans to increase US investment into Africa, these Hubs have broadened their mandate to include new capabilities in fostering links between US investor and African opportunities at the firm, project and sectoral level. Just this month, USAID led a group of US pension fund investors to Africa and will organize a reverse mission to the US later in the year.

The Future of US investment into Africa

Africa will be the population center of the planet over the next two generations. The continent's population will more than double by 2050 and will be the youngest and most rapidly urbanizing on the planet with 50 cities above 5 million people. The Youth Bulge is both a threat and opportunity for Africa. If properly harnessed, it can provide both a workforce and a consumer market. If not, it can be the font of desperate emigration, civic unrest and terrorism. While the US has fallen behind China and South Africa as the continent's leading investment partner, we can develop win-win strategies that provide attractive returns to US investors and economic and political stability for Africans.

Among the tools that I recommend be deployed to support increased US investment into Africa include the following:

1. Increase Market size— Many American companies are dissuaded by most African national market sizes. Sure, Nigeria, South Africa and Kenya are appealing in their own

right but Togo, Benin and Malawi may not. Fostering regional integration though bilateral and multilateral technical assistance will create scale and incentivize US firms to take a closer look. But regional integration should also be for investors and not just traders. US technical assistance to Africa's regional economic communities (EAS, COMESA, ECOWAS, SADC, SACU) and business associations can foster trade facilitation and enlarge market opportunities for US investors. For example, P&G manufactures consumer products for African's middle class but the scale of initial investment in manufacturing facilities necessities regional market access. Last, as noted below, China is making investments to improve both national and regional transportation linkages. In so doing, they are expanding markets in Africa and opportunities for US trade and investment.

2. Enhance US investment in African infrastructure – As I have testified before this committee in the past, MCC is a program that has many benefits. First, it requires accountability and commitment from recipient countries. MCC has been able to improve power supply and transportation infrastructure in targeted countries and it has encouraged improvements in the business enabling environment and human skills development, especially among youth and women. However, MCC could do more leveraging and create more targeted infrastructure investment. Along with regional compacts, MCC should consider allocating a portion of its compacts for sub-national infrastructure investment. As in the US, subnational infrastructure development creates a closer link between the user and sponsor. This will lead to greater accountability and sounder decisions and Africa has financial space to incur such debt relative to other regions. In association with ratings agencies, MCC could develop a set of criteria and operating rules for towns, cities, provinces and then provide guarantees to support local currency denominated bonds that could be purchased by national, Africa or even US and European pension funds, institutional investors and family offices.

3. Strengthen Africa's business enabling and innovation environment - While Africa has been burdened by a brain drain and a collapse of educational institutions, in many countries there has been an explosion in innovation, partly enabled by the boom in the internet. Kenya has become a global Fintech capital, Nigeria's film industry trails only the US and India in production and South Africa has research universities that are working with firms to create pan-Africa solutions in health, agriculture and education. However, innovation cannot be top down. A proper enabling environment must be evolved which offers financial and tax incentives along with strong IPR protection and judicial systems for dispute resolution and contract enforcement. Again, working on the regional level to inculcate innovation should be a target. There may be ways in which countries can share their innovative comparative advantages across borders. For example, Botswana may have a labor pool for certain automotive component manufacturing or 3D printing that might be prohibitively expensive in South Africa. But the latter has Original Equipment Manufacturers that will need support from national and neighboring South Africa Customs Union suppliers. This is already occurring. The business enabling environment is also key. There is an increase in private equity (PE)

investment into Africa and this will only increase if Africa countries continue to modernize its financial institutions and regulations. Few Americans are aware that South Africa's Johannesburg Stock Exchange is among the oldest exchanges in the world. However, the remainder of African exchanges are weak and limit the ability of PE investors to exit their investments. USAID and US Treasury can provide technical assistance and outreach to US exchanges, ratings agencies and law firms to speed the development of capital markets.

4. Foster linkages between US and Africa firms, business associations. Mark Zuckerburg recently toured Nigeria and commented that it reminded him of what Silicon Valley looked like 20 years ago. Last year I participated in the Global Entrepreneurship Summit at Stanford University and witnessed an extraordinary exchange of ideas and energy among entrepreneurs from the US and across the globe. Additionally, each year the Biological Industry Organization hosts an annual confenence in which African entrepreneurs, research institutions and government agencies are invited to share their ideas with US investors. The annual AGOA Forum rotates between Africa and the US. This annual event provides an opportunity for African business and civil society organizations to offer their observations on how trade capacity development assistance and government policies can accelerate trade, investment and economic inclusion. Last, I have been a speaker and mentor to the Young Africa Leaders Initiative's Mandela Fellows since inception. 1,000 YALI fellows are chosen each year from tens of thousands of applicants and spend several weeks in the US interacting with research universities, companies and US Citizens. YALI along with other educational exchanges foster the types of linkages and understanding that provide benefits well into the future and represent good value for public diplomacy. I should also note the growing importance of the Africa diaspora in the US in serving as a link to innovation, trade and investment. Often these linkages are facilitated by national (CCA, IGD, BCIU and US Chamber) and regional (Africa Chamber of Commerce of the Pacific Northwest) business organizations.

5. Maintain US instruments at OPIC, EXIM and TDA. In a perfect world, such risk mitigating instruments as OPIC, EXIM and TDA would not be needed to facilitate US Trade and investment, Regrettably, we do not live in a perfect world. When I began my commercial career in Africa nearly four decades ago, the usual lament from US firms were the subsidies and non-transparent business practices of our European competitors. Today those complaints are directed at China. In 2015 alone, China extended over $500 billion in export credits whereas EXIM extended $10 billion. When Africans engage with the US, it is over the absence of US FDI and not for increases in development assistance. OPIC plays and important role in incentivizing US FDI without crowding out the private sector, especially into high risk countries. And OPIC provides a profit to the US Treasury and according to the Center for Global Development, only 8% of its services are used by Fortune 500 companies. TDA is a small and useful agency that can directly trace its activities to increase US exports of goods and services and jobs and EXIM Bank is a proven and effective means to support exports and jobs.

6. Maintain USFCS, FAS and domestic USEAC offices – Such Blue Chips companies as Caterpillar, GE, Merck and Boeing have long established presences in Africa. Small and medium sized US companies have much to offer Africa but are inexperienced and often reluctant to participate in Africa growing market place. For example, Africa has the largest portion of undeveloped arable land in the work and US agribusiness firms offer a suite of products and service that could actualize that potential. There is no possibility for Africa to feed itself without undergoing a technological transformation as happened in India in the Green Revolution. The Foreign Agricultural Service has traditionally been focused on supported US agricultural commodity exports. However, the bigger opportunity lies with US companies to provides good, technology and services. The US Department of Commerce also has an important role in (1) informing these small and medium sized form of the opportunities in Africa and (2) having FCS offices support US firms and business missions when they travel to Africa.

Mr. Carroll is also Vice President of Manchester Trade Ltd., and founding director of Acorus Capital, an Africa focused private equity fund.

Chairman ROYCE. Thank you, Tony.
Ambassador Brigety?

STATEMENT OF THE HONORABLE REUBEN E. BRIGETY II, DEAN, ELLIOTT SCHOOL OF INTERNATIONAL AFFAIRS, THE GEORGE WASHINGTON UNIVERSITY (FORMER U.S. REPRESENTATIVE TO THE AFRICAN UNION, U.S. DEPARTMENT OF STATE)

Ambassador BRIGETY. Chairman Royce, Ranking Member Engel, Chairman Smith, Ranking Member Bass, distinguished members of the committee, good morning. My name is Ambassador Reuben Brigety. I am the dean of the Elliott School of International Affairs at the George Washington University. Thank you very much for inviting me to testify this morning regarding U.S. interests in Africa.

In my view, the bases of U.S. engagement with Africa in the near future should largely remain what they have been over the last three decades over both Republican and Democratic administrations. They include a commitment to broadening democratic governance, cooperating on matters of mutual security, strengthening healthcare systems, and supporting economic development. I have elaborated at length about U.S. priorities in Africa in an article entitled, "The New Pan-Africanism: Implications for U.S. Policy in Africa," which was published in the journal, Survival, in the summer of 2016. I submit this article for the record.

Chairman ROYCE. Without objection.

Ambassador BRIGETY. However, I would like to use the bulk of my testimony this morning to emphasize that U.S. objectives in Africa cannot be realized with the dramatic and draconian cuts to the U.S. Department of State and the U.S. Agency for International Development which have been proposed by the Trump administration. In the Office of Management and Budgets' document, America First: A Budget Blueprint to Make America Great Again, President Trump proposes "deep cuts to foreign aid."

The President's 2018 budget request for the Department of State and USAID proposed a staggering 28 percent reduction from the 2017 annualized continuing resolution level. Recent media reports suggest that Secretary of State Tillerson plans to have a reduction of 2,300 foreign and civil service officers, or nearly 10 percent of the State Department's professional work force, within the next 2 years.

Mr. Chairman, let me say clearly and emphatically that such deep cuts to the Department of State and USAID budgets will cause unavoidable damage to African partners and to American interests on the continent. The presumption by the White House and the Secretary of State that the ranks of the Foreign Service can be dramatically reduced without harming the national interests of the United States is incorrect, particularly as it relates to Africa.

As a former United States Ambassador to the African Union and former Deputy Assistant Secretary of State for Africa, I can attest to the fact that diplomacy in Africa is a retail business, perhaps more so than in other parts of the world. Engaging directly and repeatedly with government officials, business people, and civic leaders is essential for building trust, gathering information, and advancing policies.

It is self-evident that decreasing the number of diplomats available to serve in U.S. Embassies abroad, to include Africa, will decrease our ability to shape events and advance our interests on the continent. This is made all the more problematic because U.S. Embassies in Africa are already understaffed relative to our diplomatic missions in Europe.

From Nouakchott to Nairobi, many circumstances exist to a greater or lesser degree at U.S. Embassies across sub-Saharan Africa where a relatively small number of diplomats compared, for example, to our diplomatic footprint in Riga or Berlin, must work exceptionally hard to develop the relationships needed to advance U.S. interests. Whether it be finding a way to end the fighting in South Sudan or facilitating an eventual political transition in Zimbabwe, it is impossible to foresee how decreasing our diplomatic presence in Africa can contribute to those and other important objectives.

The problem is perhaps even more tangible as it relates to proposed cuts to the USAID budget. With the breadth of challenges and scope of opportunities on the continent today, cutting the USAID budget will inevitably harm African partners and hurt American interests. It is self-evident that massive cuts to the USAID budget, inevitably leading to the closure of USAID missions and the depletion of vital programs, will cripple our ability to respond to these and other pressing challenges.

Mr. Chairman, when I served as the U.S. Ambassador to the African Union, I proudly often said that the United States was "the natural partner of choice for Africa." If such draconian cuts to the Department of State and USAID are allowed to proceed, then we will abdicate our position of principled partnership with African governments. We will, in effect, have gift-wrapped the continent and handed it to China. We must not cede our position of partnership to China, which would surely happen if the Trump administration's damaging budget proposals are adopted.

In conclusion, I commend the committee for examining the important issue of U.S. interests of Africa, and let me say as well that maintaining the capacity of USAID and the State Department to continue to engage is squarely in the interest of our country. Thank you very much. I look forward to your questions.

[The prepared statement of Ambassador Brigety follows:]

Congressional Testimony before the
House Foreign Affairs Committee
"U.S. Interests in Africa"
Ambassador (ret.) Reuben E. Brigety, II
Dean, Elliott School of International Affairs
The George Washington University
May 18, 2017

Good morning, Chairman Royce, Ranking Member Engel and members of this committee. My name is Ambassador (ret.) Reuben E. Brigety, II and I am the Dean of the Elliott School of International Affairs at The George Washington University. I thank you all very much for inviting me to testify before the committee today regarding "U.S. Interests in Africa."

In my view, the bases of U.S. engagement with Africa in the near future should largely remain what they have been over the last three decades under both Republican and Democratic administrations. They include a commitment to broadening democratic governance, cooperating on matters of mutual security, strengthening healthcare systems and supporting economic development. I have elaborated at length about U.S. priorities in Africa in an article entitled "The New Pan-Africanism – Implications for U.S. Policy in Africa" published in the journal *Survival* in the summer of 2016. I submit the article to the record.

However, I would like to use the bulk of my testimony to emphasize that U.S. objectives in Africa cannot be realized with the dramatic and draconian cuts to the United States Department of State and to the United States Agency for International Development (USAID) which have been proposed by the Trump Administration.

In the Office of Management and Budget's document "America First: A Budget Blueprint to Make America Great Again," President Trump proposes "deep cuts to foreign aid." The President's 2018 budget request for the Department of State and USAID propose a staggering 28% reduction from the 2017 annualized continuing resolution (CR) level. Recent media reports suggest that Secretary of State Tillerson plans to have a reduction of 2,300 foreign and civil service officers, or nearly 10% of the State Department's workforce, within the next two years.

Mr. Chairman, let me say clearly and emphatically that such deep cuts to the Department of State and USAID budgets will cause unavoidable damage to African partners and to American interests on the continent. The presumption by the White House and the Secretary of State that the ranks of the Foreign Service can be dramatically reduced without harming the national interests of the United States is incorrect, particularly as it relates to Africa. As a former U.S. Ambassador to the African Union and a former Deputy Assistant Secretary of State for Africa, I can attest to the fact that diplomacy in Africa is a retail business. Perhaps more so than in other parts of the world, engaging directly and repeatedly with government officials, business people, and civic leaders is essential for building trust, gathering information, and advancing policies. It is self-evident that decreasing the number of diplomats available to serve in U.S. Embassies abroad (to include in Africa) will decrease our ability to shape events and advance our interests on the continent.

This is made all the more problematic because U.S. Embassies in Africa are already understaffed relative to our diplomatic missions in Europe. For example, when I was the Chief of Mission for the U.S. Mission to the African Union from 2013-2015, I never had more than four State Department Foreign Service Officers assigned to me at any given time. This was for a mission that was responsible for engaging a multilateral organization with 54 (at the time) sovereign members in Addis Ababa, the capital city of Ethiopia that hosted over 120 diplomatic missions – any one of which could have been important for our country to engage at any given time. From Nouakchott to Nairobi, similar circumstances exist to a greater or lesser degree at U.S. Embassies across sub-Saharan Africa, where a relatively small number of diplomats (compared to our diplomatic footprint in Riga or Berlin, for example) must work exceptionally hard to develop the relationships needed to advance U.S. interests. Whether it be finding a way to end the fighting in South Sudan or facilitating an eventual political transition in Zimbabwe, it is impossible to foresee how *decreasing* our diplomatic presence in Africa can contribute to those and other important objectives.

The problem is perhaps even more tangible as it relates to proposed cuts to the USAID budget. Advancing historically bipartisan U.S. objectives of democratic governance, humanitarian response, health, education, and economic development in Africa necessarily requires programmatic funds. With the breadth of challenges and scope of opportunities on the continent today, cutting the USAID budget will inevitably harm African partners and hurt American interests. The emerging trend of "constitutional coups" whereby long-serving leaders alter their constitutional arrangements to hold on to power threatens fragile democratic norms in Africa. As we sit here today, the world faces four current/near famines, three of which are in Africa. Further, Ebola is resurgent in the Democratic Republic of the Congo. The so-called "Youth Bulge" of dynamic but restive young people across Africa is coming of age, eager for work and education at home but willing to migrate across dangerous seas if necessary to build their futures. It is self-evident that massive cuts to the USAID budget, inevitably leading to the closure of USAID missions and the depletion of vital program funds, will cripple our ability to respond to these and other pressing challenges on the continent.

When I was the U.S. Ambassador to the African Union, I said, the United States was the "natural partner of choice for Africa." This was not only because we shared both a common history and common interests, but also because the United States was a leading partner with African governments on a host of issues, from battling the HIV/AIDS pandemic to fostering economic growth.

If such draconian cuts to the Department of State and USAID budgets are allowed to proceed, then we will abdicate our position of principled partnership with African governments. We will, in effect, have gift-wrapped the continent and handed it to China. As has been widely reported, the Chinese have increased their diplomatic presence across Africa even as they have invested heavily in a variety of infrastructure projects on the continent. While there may be a coincidence of interests between the Chinese and American views of economic development in Africa, our agendas diverge sharply regarding our diplomatic motives and our priorities for democratic governance. We must not cede our position of partnership to China, which would surely happen if the Trump Administration's damaging budget proposals are adopted.

In conclusion, I commend the committee for examining the important issue of "U.S. Interests in Africa," an area of the world that has enjoyed broad bipartisan support and consensus over much of the last thirty years. Continuing robust engagement in Africa in the near term is squarely in the interests of the United States. Maintaining the capacity of the Department of State and USAID continue that engagement is also squarely in the interests of our country. Thank you.

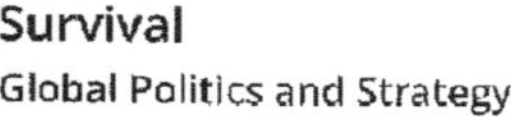

Survival

Global Politics and Strategy

Routledge
Taylor & Francis Group

ISSN: 0039-6338 (Print) 1468-2699 (Online) Journal homepage: http://www.tandfonline.com/loi/tsur20

The New Pan-Africanism: Implications for US Africa Policy

Reuben E. Brigety II

To cite this article: Reuben E. Brigety II (2016) The New Pan-Africanism: Implications for US Africa Policy, Survival, 58:4, 159-176, DOI: 10.1080/00396338.2016.1186985

To link to this article: http://dx.doi.org/10.1080/00396338.2016.1186985

Published online: 19 Jul 2016.

Submit your article to this journal

Article views: 521

View related articles

View Crossmark data

The New Pan-Africanism: Implications for US Africa Policy

Reuben E. Brigety, II

The idea that Africa, a continent shared by more than 50 states with unique histories, cultures and interests, could be more than the sum of its parts dates back at least as far as May 1963, when an emerging sense of a common African destiny led the leaders of free Africa to gather in Addis Ababa, Ethiopia, to create the Organisation of African Unity. Almost 40 years later, a similar feeling of pan-African identity led to the founding of the African Union (AU). A sense of continental solidarity can be seen in cultural products such as the poetry of Léopold Senghor and the songs of Miriam Makeba, and in the behaviour of African states in multilateral forums such as the UN General Assembly and the World Trade Organisation. The tendency for states to adopt and adhere to common African positions (as they did in the negotiations for the Sustainable Development Goals, the Bali round of World Trade Organisation negotiations and the Ezulwini Consensus on UN Security Council reform) reflects an understanding of – and a commitment to – a set of particularly African interests that are best pursued collectively rather than individually. The persistence of nationalistic rivalries among, and the pursuit of divergent policies by, African states is not necessarily evidence that pan-Africanism has no political merit or consequence, any more than differences in policies or the persistence of tensions among European nations represent an indictment of the idea of Europe. Rather, it merely demonstrates the complexity of African states' foreign policies as they try to

Reuben E. Brigety, II, is the Dean of the Elliott School of International Affairs at the George Washington University. From 2013 to 2015 he was the US Representative to the African Union and US Permanent Representative to the UN Economic Commission for Africa.

Survival | vol. 58 no. 4 | August–September 2016 | pp. 159–176   DOI 10.1080/00396338.2016.1186985

advance their interests both unilaterally, on the basis of their own national capabilities, and multilaterally, under the banner of African solidarity.

If the idea of 'Africa' has genuine purchase in international affairs, can the United States see Africa as a strategic partner? To answer this question, it is useful to look at what a strategic partner is. In recent years there has been a proliferation of strategic partnerships between the United States and other countries and entities. Today, the US has four such partnerships within Africa alone: with Angola, Nigeria, South Africa and the AU Commission.

A strategic partnership is a customary arrangement or formal agreement between two polities (such as a sovereign state or a multilateral organisation) to engage regularly in purposeful dialogue and to pursue mutual interests together over time. The strength of a strategic partnership depends on three elements: the breadth and coincidence of the partners' enduring interests; the degree of trust in the relationship; and the capacity of each party to apply resources for the advancement of their shared interests. The relationships that the United States enjoys with the United Kingdom and NATO exemplify the gold standard of strategic partnerships. Conversely, the failure of Washington's attempted 'reset' in relations with Moscow shows how clashing interests and mutual mistrust can limit a would-be partnership. What, then, are the current elements of, and future prospects for, a strategic partnership between the United States and Africa?

The elements of partnership

To begin with, the United States and Africa share common interests. The most recent articulation of US interests with regard to Africa can be found in President Barack Obama's strategy for sub-Saharan Africa. The strategy is based on four pillars: strengthening democratic institutions; spurring economic growth, trade and investment; advancing peace and security; and promoting opportunity and development.[1] Each of these areas of interest has been pursued in Africa as a matter of stated policy or actual practice by every US administration – both Republican and Democratic – since the end of the Cold War. Even more significantly, they are consistent with what Africa says it wants for itself.

With regard to democratic governance, the Constitutive Act of the African Union explicitly calls for 'respect for democratic principles, human rights, the rule of law and good governance',[2] as well as 'condemnation and rejection of unconstitutional changes of government'.[3] There is alignment on economic priorities as well, since virtually all African states have abandoned the socialist and Marxist economic models that many adopted shortly after they gained independence. Most now want to expand their private sectors, as evidenced by (among other indicators) the unanimous call by African states for the swift renewal of the African Growth and Opportunity Act (AGOA) by the US Congress in 2015.[4] On matters of peace and security, African states have made strong political declarations in favour of achieving a conflict-free Africa by 2020, and many have placed their own soldiers in harm's way to serve in AU and UN peacekeeping missions across the continent. The priority areas that African countries have defined for their own opportunity and development – improving food security, strengthening tertiary education, building climate-resilient communities and the like – directly align with the global-development agenda of the United States.

The picture is, of course, more mixed when one examines actual practice. In the area of democracy and governance, there is a significant gap not only between the interests professed by the United States and the realities of African life, but also (and more importantly) between what Africans say they want and how they are actually governed. Freedom House argues that Africa 'saw overall if uneven progress toward democratization in the 1990s and early 2000s. However recent years have seen backsliding among both the top performers … and the more repressive countries.'[5] It considers only 20% of the countries and territories in sub-Saharan Africa to be fully free, and just 37% to be partially free.[6]

Economically, the picture is better, but significant improvement is still needed. Sub-Saharan Africa as a whole experienced an average annual GDP growth rate of 5.2% over the last five years, and is home to seven of the ten fastest-growing economies in the world.[7] In the last 15 years, the value of US exports to Africa has grown by an average of 11.3% annually, or by more than 300% over that period.[8] Nevertheless, protectionist trading policies adopted by African states continue to inhibit economic growth, with less than 2% of all African trade occurring internally. At the same time, corruption has served to constrain American foreign direct investment. The US Foreign Corrupt Practices Act appropriately punishes American business-people who would seek to contribute to the more than $52 billion in illicit financial transactions involving Africa every year,[9] causing many legitimate American businesses to avoid the continent – perceived to be rife with corruption – for fear of running afoul of the law.

There have been successes in ending deadly conflicts in Africa (such as the civil wars in Liberia, Angola, Mozambique and Sierra Leone), even as new conflicts have arisen in their stead, in places such as Central African Republic (CAR), South Sudan and the Lake Chad Basin. As conflicts have ebbed and flowed, the capacity of African regional and continental organisations to address them has increased. AU peacekeepers have played pivotal roles in Somalia, Mali and CAR, operating on a shoestring compared to relatively well-financed UN missions. Yet important decisions remain to be made and implemented by the AU regarding the financing of a standing African military capability.

With regard to broad issues of opportunity and development, a significant gap between needs and resources remains, as do differences between Africa and donor countries on how to address it. Even as Africa calls on G7 members to fulfil their pledge to commit 0.7% of their GDP to official development assistance,[10] Organisation for Economic Co-operation and Development (OECD) countries are increasingly calling on developing countries, including those in Africa, to more effectively mobilise domestic resources in pursuit of their own development.[11]

Yet despite these gaps, there is substantial overlap between the outcomes sought by the United States and Africa for the continent. This consensus could certainly serve as the basis for a strategic partnership. Moreover, any differences between policy and practice are due less to a fundamental divergence in the interests of the two sides than they are to challenges of implementation or discrete political circumstances.

What of the extent of trust between the US and Africa? For both sides, perceptions and behaviour have been greatly influenced by two key historical events, the Cold War and the liberation struggle. There is, of course, overlap and interplay between the two periods, both of which have done much to shape the complexities of the relationship. Like elsewhere in the world, US engagement in Africa for most of the second half of the twentieth century was heavily influenced, if not outright defined, by its Cold War competition with the Soviet Union. US policies in Africa and elsewhere were designed less to support democratic institutions and more to cultivate supporters and check Soviet clients. This led to some unsavoury associations – with South African apartheid and Mobutu Sese Seko's Zaire, for instance – that are hard to defend today. At roughly the same time, much of Africa was agitating for independence from its colonial masters, either through diplomacy or through force of arms. Many Africans believed that, by prioritising its Cold War competition over legitimate African aspirations for freedom, the United States was on the wrong side of history. This belief remains entrenched among members of Africa's liberation generation, many of whom now hold power. It has fed suspicion of US motives for the intervention in Libya, the Young African Leaders Initiative and the US Africa Command.[12]

Africans are willing to embrace American leaders who stand with them

Despite this history of suspicion, Africans are willing to embrace American leaders who stand with them. President George W. Bush is widely praised for the life-saving President's Emergency Plan for AIDS Relief, and lauded for creating a new model of development assistance through the Millennium Challenge Corporation. President Obama was rapturously welcomed during his July 2015 visit to Kenya and praised for his tough-love speech at AU headquarters calling for African leaders to observe term limits and respect their constitutions. Africans are also avid consumers of American culture. One can hear American hip-hop music, or African versions of it, on virtually every radio station on the continent, and Jay-Z and Beyoncé are as well known in Nairobi and Lagos as they are in New York and Los Angeles. Finally, many African political and business leaders completed a portion of their studies at US universities, giving them an understanding of (and even an affinity for) American culture.

Notwithstanding leftover suspicions from the Cold War, the bonds of trust between the United States and Africa are growing and could serve as the basis for a stronger future relationship.

Does Africa have the capacity to bring unique capabilities to a strategic relationship with the United States? The answer, again, depends on the area under consideration. In the realm of peace and security, the answer is a resounding 'yes'. What African states have lacked in financial resources and material capability they have made up for in their willingness to fight and in their bravery under fire. Somalia today has a civilian government for the first time in a generation due to the willingness of forces from Uganda, Burundi, Ethiopia, Kenya and Djibouti to do battle with al-Shabaab under the banner of the AU Mission in Somalia (AMISOM) even during some of the darkest days of the conflict. AU troops have proven willing, and decisive, in addressing crises in CAR and Mali, and are engaging Boko Haram as part of a multinational effort. On matters of democracy and governance, however, the picture is more mixed. African continental and regional diplomatic missions have proven essential in countering the coup in Burkina Faso and in encouraging respect for democratic processes in Nigeria. Yet the challenges of regional politics have made it harder for African institutions to encourage – or demand – respect for constitutional limits or clean electoral processes in Burundi, Zimbabwe and elsewhere. The capacity for partnership is arguably weakest in matters of economic growth, trade and investment. Even though bilateral trade between the United States and Africa has grown dramatically over the last 15 years, the continent has thus far proven itself incapable of decisively addressing the greatest barriers to improved economic cooperation by, inter alia, confronting corruption, building multinational markets of scale, and ensuring transparency and respect for the rule of law consistent with international business standards.

It is clear that there is a convergence of interests, a sufficient degree of trust and the collective capacity to establish a strategic partnership between the United States and Africa. Such a partnership holds the potential to help define the twenty-first century. Many of the challenges that will confront the international community in the coming decades – adaptation to climate change, ensuring peace and security in an age of violent non-state actors, ending extreme poverty and expanding economic opportunity – are at play in Africa. To solve them, the United States needs Africa as a whole, in addition to individual countries, to be a willing, capable and dependable partner.

Building partnership

There are at least four ways, in addition to current initiatives, in which the US could advance the project of African unity in a manner that would support both sides' interests: by actively supporting the idea of pan-African unity; by substantially increasing financial, material and technical support for African democratic institutions; by involving the US private sector to an even greater extent; and by improving problematic US bilateral relationships on the continent.

Supporting pan-African unity

The achievement of a peaceful, prosperous and integrated Africa is the *raison d'être* of the AU and a goal that enjoys unanimous rhetorical support across the continent. Given the strength of this political ideal, the United States should be a proactive advocate of pan-African unity. Many (if not most) Africans would interpret such a position as American support for the destiny that Africans have chosen for themselves. This would likely improve levels of trust in American motives among the African political class. Moreover, American support for goals that Africans have already made a rhetorical commitment to (such as respect for human rights, democracy and economic prosperity) could be a powerful statement on the convergence of American and African interests. Conversely, US ambivalence or hostility toward pan-African unity can only fuel mistrust about American motives on the continent and limit the possibilities for the United States to influence its political development.

As the institutional project of building African unity proceeds apace, a debate has emerged within US policy circles about whether a stronger and more united Africa is good for America. On the one hand, an Africa that can speak more authoritatively about its own interests and that can enforce its own standards on matters such as economic integration and respect for human rights could be a powerful ally of the United States for the advancement of mutual interests both in Africa and beyond. On the other hand, there is a legitimate fear that a more united Africa could act against US priorities, as it did, for example, in 2013–14 with its rejection of International Criminal Court jurisdiction over sitting African heads of state, or as it might by supporting adversarial Chinese or Russian positions in the UN Security Council and elsewhere.

This debate resembles similar discussions in the 1990s concerning how a strengthened European Union might affect American interests in Europe and beyond. On balance, in the nearly 25 years since the signing of the Maastricht Treaty, it has become clear that a strong EU has been good for American interests as well. Any differences between the US and the EU on matters such as World Trade Organisation disputes or the wisdom of the 2003 Iraq War have been overshadowed by the strong cooperation they have demonstrated in other areas, such as in jointly fighting piracy off the Horn of Africa and in responding to the Ebola crisis of 2014.

A similar dynamic could develop between the US and Africa. A generation from now, the project of African unity could be both far more advanced than it is today and demonstrably beneficial for both US and African interests. Achieving this result will require consistent rhetorical support from American foreign-policy leaders for the pan-African ideal. At the same time, it will also require specific policy initiatives to advance regional integration on the continent.

For example, the US should allow multiple African countries to submit joint project proposals for funding by the Millennium Challenge Corporation (MCC) that would advance the integration of regional markets through the construction of transnational highways or multinational manufacturing parks. This would facilitate the creation of regional markets with the necessary scale and scope to more readily attract US foreign direct investment. Currently, only individual countries can apply for MCC compacts, and their success in winning them depends on the 'scorecard' they receive from the MCC on key governance indicators, such as ruling justly, investing in people and encouraging economic freedom. If multiple countries were able to submit joint proposals for MCC funding, there would be productive pressure from all of the applicant nations on each other to achieve the threshold standard of the MCC governance indicators. This would not only be a tangible tool for the United States to encourage strong governance in support of pan-African Unity, but the projects themselves would enhance regional economic integration to the benefit of both African countries and American companies seeking to do business with them.

In addition, the United States should substantially strengthen its diplomatic engagement with the eight regional economic communities (RECs) that form the building blocks for the political organisation of the continent. In most cases, the United States accredits its resident ambassadors to the countries in which the RECs are based as representatives to the RECs themselves. For example, the US ambassador to Botswana is also dually accredited as the US representative to the Southern African Development Community (SADC), the headquarters of which is in Gaborone. Yet the duties of these US representatives concerning the RECs are at best of secondary importance given that, in most cases, there is no formal political framework to advance the mutual interests of the United States and the REC in question. Conversely, the United States and the AU Commission have a formal agreement that has helped strengthen their partnership, culminating in the visit by President Obama to the AU headquarters in Addis Ababa in July 2015. A concerted effort to invigorate and deepen the political dialogue with the RECs would expand the reservoir of trust between Africa and the US, identify tangible initiatives for strengthening regional integration that could be pursued jointly, and improve US understanding of regional dynamics that affect continent-wide challenges.

Increasing support for African democratic institutions

Although Africa's political commitment to democratic governance is strong, its institutions to support democratic governance are relatively weak. Understaffed and underfunded, entities such as the AU's Department for Political Affairs (which is charged with vital functions such as election monitoring and political mediation) could be important drivers for strengthening democratic governance on the continent. Yet both African states and external partners alike have invested far more heavily in the continent's security architecture (such as in AU peacekeeping missions) than they have in Africa's governance structures.

The long-term economic growth and political stability of Africa is dependent on its ability to solidify still-fragile and uneven gains in democratic governance in accordance with its commitments. It will be challenging at best, however, for Africa to achieve this result on its own. Though several African countries, including Ghana, Mauritius and South Africa, have established strong democratic political cultures, there is no democratic centre of gravity on the continent that can meaningfully exert positive pressure on less democratic countries to improve their governance. In contrast, the prospect of enjoying the economic prosperity and political freedoms of the EU (as well as the requirement to implement the EU's *acquis communautaire*, or body of laws) were powerful incentives for the former communist countries of Eastern Europe to reform their political systems in line with the requirements for EU membership. In this case, the established democracies of Western and Central Europe exerted a kind of gravitational pull to help the newly independent countries of Eastern Europe accelerate and solidify their commitment to democratic governance.

In the absence of such a democratic centre of gravity in Africa, the best alternative is for external partners to strengthen democratic institutions through financial assistance and technical support. The AU Commission, and in particular its departments of political affairs and of peace and security (which has responsibility for continental early warning and conflict mediation) have shown a keen willingness to support democracy in Africa in a manner consistent with AU declarations and statements of principle. For example, the Department of Political Affairs played an important role in the Nigerian elections of March 2015, working assiduously behind the scenes to convince both parties to ensure a free and fair voting process, and to accept the ultimate outcome. Due in no small part to this proactive diplomacy, Nigeria experienced the first peaceful transfer of power from an incumbent president to an electoral challenger in its history. Similarly, the Department of Peace and Security, as well as the Peace and Security Council, moved swiftly to condemn the military coup in Burkina Faso in September 2015, emphasising that the seizure of power by force and unconstitutional changes of government were unacceptable.[13] Yet there have also been recent setbacks. Months of quiet diplomacy by senior AU officials could not convince Burundian President Pierre Nkurunziza to stand down from his bid for a third term, in clear violation of the Arusha Accords, particularly as he received support from some heads of state in Central and Eastern Africa who were likewise poised to seek unconstitutional third terms in office. In addition, the AU, as the only external organisation invited to monitor the most recent federal elections in Ethiopia in June 2015, stunningly declared the process 'to be calm, peaceful, and credible as it provided an opportunity for the Ethiopian people to express their choices at the polls', despite the fact that the ruling party won 100% of the seats in parliament.[14]

To improve the ability of African institutions to advance democratic governance on the continent, the United States and its like-minded donor partners should propose a substantial support package at both the continental and regional levels that identifies the most promising institutions with which to work on democratic governance, that develops jointly with African stakeholders action plans to strengthen those institutions, and that makes multi-year commitments of financial resources and technical assistance to implement those plans. It is vital that the United States take the lead in this initiative, given its belief in the efficacy of democratic institutions for social stability and prosperity. African concerns about American hegemony, however, mean that it is equally important that such an initiative include a mixture of donors with similar commitments to democracy (such as the EU, Japan, Australia, India and Brazil), and that it be carried out in close cooperation with African multilateral organisations themselves.

If this democracy-building project were successful, Africa could well become the largest democratic region in the world. A generation ago, few would have predicted that most of Moscow's Warsaw Pact allies would one day be part of a democratic Europe, or that almost all of Latin America would be governed by freely elected leaders rather than unaccountable despots. Africa has the potential to be the world's next democratic success story, but both the continent and its partners will need to take specific actions to realise this vision.

Engaging the US private sector

Private-sector-led economic growth will be vital to writing Africa's next chapter. The security and prosperity of the continent depend on the generation of enough jobs to employ more than 200 million young people intent on building their futures. For most African leaders, the prospect of large numbers of unemployed young people is not simply an economic challenge, but also a political and societal threat. As such, US political influence in Africa will likely depend at least as much on economic linkages with African economies as on political ties to African governments. The United States, therefore, has a vital economic and political interest in facilitating the entry of American businesses into virtually every sector of Africa's economy. At the same time, opportunities for American firms to engage in profitable enterprises in Africa are multiplying as many African economies continue to expand, and as labour in Asia becomes more expensive.

In recent years, the US government has taken a number of steps to facilitate American business involvement in Africa. For instance, at the August 2014 African Leaders Summit in Washington, the US government's Doing Business in Africa Campaign announced over \$33bn in new commitments to support economic growth in Africa. The US Department of Commerce has increased the number of Foreign Commercial Service officers on the continent, and opened an office in Addis Ababa – the diplomatic capital of Africa.[15] The Overseas Private Investment Corporation (OPIC) has nearly quadrupled its investments in Africa in the last decade, financing around \$4bn in projects.[16] And Power Africa, President Obama's signature initiative, has involved dozens of American companies in supporting the objective of adding 30,000 megawatts of reliable energy-generating capacity for the continent.[17]

Nevertheless, more could be done, particularly in the area of non-energy infrastructure development. In January 2012, the AU's Assembly of Heads of State and Government adopted the Program for Infrastructure Development in Africa (PIDA).[18] PIDA is a collection of over 50 projects across sectors (such as transportation, telecommunications, trans-boundary water resources and energy) designed to support economic development in Africa by strengthening regional and continental access to sound infrastructure. Establishing mechanisms for American firms to profitably engage in PIDA projects would simultaneously support several US interests as once. Firstly, it would be a strong signal that the United States is an active proponent of regional and continental integration consistent with the vision that Africa has adopted for itself. Secondly, it could enhance Washington's long-term political influence in Africa as American firms helped build and operate African roads, ports and water networks, while also employing and training large numbers of African workers. Finally, the successful completion of profitable projects would benefit US companies and further strengthen US ties to African markets.

American firms participating in PIDA projects currently face two key challenges. Firstly, given the perceptions of political risk associated with doing business in Africa, and the length of time required to complete many infrastructure projects, it is very difficult for US firms to obtain project financing at rates that can compete with those enjoyed by rival firms from China and elsewhere. Secondly, concerns about the long-term stability of African regulatory regimes (or, indeed, of African governments themselves) often make US firms skittish about undertaking ambitious infrastructure projects in Africa.

Yet proactive diplomacy and skilful financing could go a long way towards overcoming both of these challenges, and the United States and African stakeholders should jointly launch an initiative to mitigate these risks. African partners could agree to issue tenders for PIDA projects that take into account more than just the cost of the project, including factors such as labour standards, training for indigenous workers and project quality – all areas in which American firms excel. In exchange, OPIC could work with private investment banks to float bonds to finance specific PIDA projects in a way that would spread the risk among potential investors and thus decrease the interest rates of the loans. OPIC could also provide political-risk insurance to assuage the concerns of firms leery of taking on longer-term construction projects in Africa. Finally, a key element of this initiative should be a structured, regular dialogue between the US government, African governmental stakeholders and American private-sector representatives to identify and address structural barriers to the competitiveness of US firms interested in participating in PIDA projects.

Resolving problematic bilateral relationships
The political importance of pan-African unity means that the nature of US bilateral relationships with individual African countries can have regional,

and even continental, ramifications. The relationship between the United States and Cuba, and its implications for American engagement in the Western Hemisphere, is an appropriate analogy. For decades, the hostile character of US–Cuban relations had a dampening effect on US relations with Latin America as a whole. Thus, a major factor in the Obama administration's calculus in normalising relations with Cuba was the positive impact that such a move would have for US standing in the entire region, in addition to the implications for the bilateral relationship.

The strength of the pan-African narrative in African politics is arguably even stronger than the call for regional solidarity in Latin America. Thus, it is essential that the United States take into account the impact of its bilateral relationships in Africa on its engagement with certain sub-regions, or indeed with the continent as a whole, and that it calibrate its diplomatic engagement accordingly. While there are a handful of US–African bilateral relationships that have regional or continental ramifications, the most important of these is with Zimbabwe.

Zimbabwe's president, Robert Mugabe, along with more than 100 individuals and some 70 legal entities, have been the subjects of targeted sanctions since 2003. The sanctions were first imposed following the seriously flawed 2002 elections, which many election observers described as marred by blatant irregularities and voter intimidation.[19] Designed to isolate those most responsible for the political violence and to pressure Zimbabwe's leadership to create a freer political environment, the sanctions have had, at best, a mixed record of success.

More problematic, however, has been the unintended impact of the sanctions on the relationship between the United States and the SADC. Harare has successfully convinced its African neighbours that the American sanctions are fundamentally unjust. To support this thesis, the Zimbabweans regularly point to the close relationships that the United States enjoys with other countries – both in Africa and beyond – that allegedly have even worse governance records than Zimbabwe. Furthermore, they have convinced their African allies that there is nothing the government of Zimbabwe could do to satisfy American demands regarding democratic norms and respect for human rights. As a result, the SADC membership (which covers the most stable and prosperous region of Africa) has rallied around Zimbabwe and made it exceedingly difficult for the United States to have a meaningful diplomatic and economic relationship with the organisation. This sentiment has spread to the rest of the continent as well. In January 2015, African heads of state elected Mugabe as the chairman of the Assembly of the AU, rather than passing him over in favour of another Southern African leader. And, in her remarks preceding Obama's historic speech to the AU in July 2015, AU Commission Chairperson Nksozana Dlamini-Zuma praised the United States for normalising its relationship with Cuba in a thinly veiled plea to do the same with Zimbabwe.

However justified the sanctions regime against Zimbabwe's anti-democratic leadership may have been at its inception, it has not succeeded in achieving its principal objective of improving the democratic climate in the country. Worse, it has impeded cooperation with the SADC, contrary to both parties' mutual interests. The United States should rethink its Zimbabwe policy and adopt prudent adjustments to achieve its desired outcome of improved governance in the country without prejudicing its relationship with Southern Africa as a whole. This should include further refinement of the list of those targeted by sanctions to include only President Mugabe and the handful of people in his entourage most responsible for the repressive climate in the country. Changes to the sanctions policy would counter the Zimbabwean narrative that there is nothing the country could do to satisfy the demands of the United States. The onus would be more clearly on Zimbabwe's senior leadership to improve governance in exchange for additional sanctions relief. And, most importantly, it would open many more possibilities for US–SADC cooperation in support of both sides' economic and political interests.

* * *

Africa is more than a collection of countries sharing the same landmass. It is also an idea, encompassing the belief that all Africans should live in harmony, prosperity and dignity. It is an idea that is no less powerful, and no less achievable, than the aspiration of the Founding Fathers of the United

States to build a country in which life, liberty and the pursuit of happiness were guaranteed to all. The current state of Africa's complex politics and myriad challenges does not render this idea invalid. Rather, Africa's problems make it all the more attractive. As the United States grapples with unprecedented global challenges in the coming decades, it will need Africa to be a partner in seeking solutions. It is therefore in the interests of the United States to work with Africans to make the idea of Africa a reality.

Notes

1. White House, 'U.S. Strategy Toward Sub-Saharan Africa', June 2012, p. 2, http://www.state.gov/documents/organization/209377.pdf.

2. 'Constitutive Act of the African Union', Article 4, paragraph (m), http://www.au.int/en/sites/default/files/ConstitutiveAct_EN.pdf.

3. *Ibid.*, paragraph (p).

4. For example, in a meeting with US Secretary of State John Kerry on 1 May 2014, Erastus Mwencha, deputy chair of the AU Commission, called for 'a seamless reauthorization for a period of at least 15 years to enable Africa's transformation with more jobs created for both Africa and the US': 'Remarks by Erastus Mwencha Deputy Chairperson, African Union Commission at the U.S.–African Union High-Level Dialogue', 1 May 2014, http://www.au.int/en/speeches/remarks-erastus-mwencha-deputy-chairperson-african-union-commission-us-african-union-high#sthash.VH1bMj4v.dpuf. President Obama signed the legislation reauthorising AGOA for ten years on 29 June 2015: Jim Kuhnhenn, 'Obama Signs Trade (Incl. AGOA), Worker Assistance Bills into Law', Associated Press, 29 June 2015, http://agoa.info/news/article/5740-obama-signs-trade-incl-agoa-worker-assistance-bills-into-law.html.

5. Freedom House, 'Sub-Saharan Africa', https://freedomhouse.org/regions/sub-saharan-africa.

6. Freedom House, 'Freedom in the World 2015', p. 17, https://freedomhouse.org/sites/default/files/01152015_FIW_2015_final.pdf.

7. 'African Economic Outlook 2015', African Economic Outlook, p. ii, http://www.africaneconomicoutlook.org/fileadmin/uploads/aeo/2015/PDF_Chapters/Overview_AEO2015_EN-web.pdf.

8. US Department of Commerce, 'US–Sub-Saharan Africa Trade and Investment', August 2014, p. 5, http://trade.gov/dbia/us-sub-saharan-africa-trade-and-investment.pdf.

9. Eleanor Whitehead, 'Illegal Financial Flows from Africa on the Rise', This Is Africa, December 2013, http://www.thisisafricaonline.com/Business/Illegal-financial-flows-from-Africa-on-the-rise.

10. Millennium Project, 'The 0.7% Target: An In-depth Look', http://www.

unmillenniumproject.org/press/07.
htm.

11   World Bank Group, 'Financing for
Development Post-2015', October
2013, pp. 16, 23, https://www.
worldbank.org/content/dam/
Worldbank/document/Poverty%20
documents/WB-PREM%20financing-
for-development-pub-10-11-13web.
pdf.

12   'US Africom "Has No Hidden
Agenda"', BBC, 1 October 2008, http://
news.bbc.co.uk/2/hi/africa/7645714.stm.

13   African Union Peace and Security,
'Communiqué of the 544th PSC
Meeting on the Situation in Burkina
Faso', 18 September 2015, http://www.
peaceau.org/en/article/communique-
of-the-544th-psc-meeting-on-the-
situation-in-burkina-faso.

14   Tetsum Berhane, 'Ethiopia Election:
Text of AU Observers' Preliminary
Report', *Horn Affairs*, 28 May 2015,
paragraph 74, http://hornaffairs.com/
en/2015/05/28/preliminary-statement-
african-union-election-observation-
mission-ethiopia/.

15   White House, 'Fact Sheet: The Doing
Business in Africa Campaign', 5
August 2015, https://www.white
house.gov/the-press-office/2014/08/05/
fact-sheet-doing-business-africa-
campaign.

16   OPIC, 'OPIC 2014 Annual Report',
https://www.opic.gov/sites/default/
files/files/opic-fy14-annual-report.
pdf.

17   US Agency for International
Development, 'Power Africa:
Annual Report 2015', p. 3, https://
www.usaid.gov/sites/default/files/
documents/1860/PA_2015_Report_
V16_TAGGING_508.pdf.

18   World Bank, 'Regional Infrastructure
in Sub-Saharan Africa: Challenges
and Opportunities', 20 February
2014, pp. 2–3, http://siteresources.
worldbank.org/1818SOCIETY/
Resources/1818AFRICApaperFINAL.
pdf.

19   Systemic Peace, 'Polity IV Country
Report 2010: Zimbabwe', http://
www.systemicpeace.org/polity/
Zimbabwe2010.pdf.

Chairman ROYCE. Thank you, Ambassador Brigety.

I am going to ask maybe three questions here dealing with poaching, dealing with trade, dealing with terrorism as it relates to State Department budget and USAID. These are programs that we have authored here, put into effect just to look at the results of them. The first I will mention to Mr. Christy here.

If we looked at the headlines 6 weeks ago, we saw China had taken the lead here on shutting down the ivory market in China. The headline was, Elephants Get Reprieve-Demand for Ivory Drops, and what was happening was the worldwide demand for ivory as a consequence of that decision, which they made after we passed the legislation, did give the species a reprieve in the sense that it dried up the demand.

Part of our legislation, besides helping on the ground with the park rangers, is the naming and shaming of those governments. You say that Sudan is a poaching "super-state" and Sudan doesn't have elephants of its own. Explain the role they are playing and what other countries you would name and shame as we put that list together, because the State Department is going to roll that out.

Mr. CHRISTY. Sudan's role as a poaching "super-state"—I use that phrase to describe what is happening with groups supported by President Omar al-Bashir, who is wanted for war crimes and crimes against humanity. His Janjaweed, whom he supports, leave on horseback from Darfur and sweep across the continent killing elephants all the way across from Chad all the way across to, in 2012, the massive killing of 650 elephants in Cameroon's Bouba N'djida Forest.

He has given home and sustenance to Joseph Kony and the Lord's Resistance Army operating in the Kafia Kingi enclave section of Darfur. The Sudanese Armed Forces are also poachers in Garamba National Park. And so unlike any other state that I am familiar with, this is government-sanctioned poaching that funds arms to these extremist groups and it is in a country that has no elephants, so it is preying upon the rest of Africa.

The naming and shaming of countries is practice that has—I don't use that phrase. But it is a practice that has achieved important results in the ivory trafficking world.

The so-called gang of eight countries that were named as ivory trafficking hotspots at the Convention on International Trade in Endangered Species had enormous effect in pressuring those countries to make a difference.

I would include those countries—I won't walk through them because I am doubtless going to miss one or two, but to them I would certainly add or include Laos, Vietnam, Thailand, and Myanmar, these countries that will take the place of China as transit countries into China as China does the admirable act of shutting down its ivory industry, I would look very significantly toward those demand countries.

Chairman ROYCE. Thank you. And that brought up a question that we should go to General Ward about and that is Joseph Kony and his Lord's Resistance Army and terrorism, the terrorization of civilians across Uganda and South Sudan and Central Africa. What is your assessment? We passed legislation here some years ago giving you and giving our U.S. military the mission of assisting in this. Give us a quick assessment if you will.

General WARD. Thank you, Mr. Chairman. The assistance that we provided to Uganda in particular, as well as other countries in the region, absolutely proved essential and provided a boost to the ability to limit the Lord's Resistance Army and Joseph Kony's ability to influence that region. It has paid off, I believe, in some very positive terms because his reach has been limited. His ability to wreak havoc in that region has been severely restricted.

It is not over. It is not done. He still is there, but his ability to do what he had been doing—especially when you look at the time frame 2008, '09, '10 and '11—has been severely reduced as a result of the support that has been provided to the African military and security forces operating in that region.

Chairman ROYCE. Thank you, General. I had one last question for Mr. Carroll. This goes to the trade issue. We passed the Electrify Africa Act here. What have you seen on the continent as far as a lack of electricity and how it impacts economic growth and how this can reverse that situation on the ground?

Mr. CARROLL. Well, I think it is of course always dangerous to make overgeneralizations. Certain countries have done a better job, a more coherent job in developing their power infrastructure, whereas other countries have fallen woefully short of the mark. Clearly, if Africa wants to expand its opportunities in manufacturing, in the growth of services sectors, which I believe it can aspire to, power is going to be an essential component of that. Power certainly alongside human resource development will be, I think, important elements of Africa's economic future.

So your efforts to not only expand U.S. corporate interests, but also—and I think it is important that we mention this, Mr. Chairman—to inspire Africans to take measures themselves to enhance and to incentivize investment in their power sector is certainly, I think, an essential step in their economic development.

Chairman ROYCE. Thank you. We go to Ranking Member Karen Bass of California.

Ms. BASS. Thank you, Mr. Chair. Thank you for holding this hearing and also for all of the witnesses and your work over the years. You know, one of the things that I have appreciated over the last couple of years in this committee is legislation like you mentioned, Electrify Africa, and also Feed the Future, which I believe begins to change the paradigm toward Africans doing for themselves.

And in that regard I wanted to ask a question both to General Ward and Ambassador Brigety. In terms of AFRICOM and U.S. military assistance to African countries, to African militaries in the AU, to increase the continent's capacity to defend itself and peacekeeping and also, you know, in a situation like what happened in Mali a couple of years ago when there was coup and they had to call in the former colonial power, they had to call in France, and so I wanted to know an assessment as to where we are and what more you think we need to do in terms of the U.S. military's assistance to the AU as well as African countries. And that is for both Ward and Brigety.

General WARD. Thank you, Congresswoman Bass. It is great to see you again. And thank you for all that you do recognizing our interests in Africa as well. I appreciate that. With respect to the role of U.S. security assistance and military assistance to the African security forces, it has made a difference. It has caused many nations on the continent to increase their professionalism and, as importantly, to improve how they operate as militaries and civilian societies abiding by the rule of law and acting in ways that are in keeping with our democratic principles with respect to the proper role of a military in a civilian society.

It is not perfect. It is not perfect. And our efforts to continue to reinforce the training that we provide, the work that is done to cause that additional professionalism to be present is certainly important. I use the term "sustained security engagement." These militaries weren't created in the way we were overnight and they won't be corrected, i.e., righted in a way that we would——

Ms. BASS. Thank you.

General WARD [continuing]. Like them to be overnight as well. So our sustained security engagement—just as is the case for sustained developmental engagement and sustained diplomatic engagement—are essential elements to continue the path that is a positive trajectory now that we see.

Ms. BASS. Thank you. Thank you. And for Ambassador Brigety?

Ambassador BRIGETY. Thank you, Congresswoman, again good to see you. From the diplomatic perspective, the most challenging aspect of African institutions providing for their own security has not been their will. Frankly, African forces have taken extraordinary risks to engage the enemy in Somalia, in the Central African Republic, and what not. The more difficult problem has been their desire and their capacity to fund themselves as well as, frankly, the politics surrounding their own particular arrangements for their own collective security.

And to answer your question about what the United States may do to further enhance that I would say two things. The good news is that as of the last AU Summit at Kigali last summer, the AU has adopted formally a number of mechanisms to help fund its own operations, broadly speaking, and then also as it relates to peacekeeping.

One of the initiatives, as you and other members of the committee will know, toward the end of the Obama administration was to partner with the African Union, which the African Union would commit within 5 years to fund 25 percent of its own peacekeeping operations so long as the United Nations would fund another 75 percent for those peacekeeping operations that were authorized by the U.N. Security Council. This is a watershed development and I would urge both Congress and the Trump administration to continue it, because in the long run it is both in the interest of the United States as well as in the interest of Africans.

The second problem set has had to do with, frankly, the political arrangements surrounding the African Standby Force, which as you will know consists of a series of five regional brigades. Politically, the difficulty within the African Union of advancing it has been some concerns among some African states that such a standing force could frankly be used as a method of regime change against other African countries.

And my own view is that the best way the United States can support that effort is to stay out of it, which is to say to let the Africans resolve that process themselves, but when they do to let them know that the United States and other organizations to which we belong, like NATO, will stand ready to be in full partnership with them to develop their military capabilities to address their own issues on the continent.

Ms. BASS. Thank you. And I ran out of time, but I would just like to ask the other two panelists maybe you could get back to me in writing, Mr. Carroll, in terms of our trade hubs, how they are working, and where else you think they need to be.

And then, Mr. Christy, you referenced the legislation that was passed last year on wildlife trafficking. I would like to know how that is working and what more you think we could do here. Thank you very much, Mr. Chair.

Chairman ROYCE. Thank you, Congresswoman Bass. We go to Chris Smith of New Jersey.

Mr. SMITH. Thank you very much, Chairman, and thank you to all of our very distinguished witnesses for your service and for your testimonies today. It is very, very helpful to all of us.

Since we only have a limited amount of time, General Ward, I would like to just discuss a couple things with you. Thank you again for being the inaugural commander, your leadership at AFRICOM. We have spoken before and it is great to see you again. I would like to ask you just two questions, two areas. The first is on the training of individuals; Leahy vetted individuals, military men and women.

In my subcommittee, the Africa Subcommittee, we tried for years to promote the training of the Nigerian military. Greg Simpkins and I, our staff director, traveled twice to Abuja. We went to Jos, where a lot of the churches have been firebombed, with Archbishop Kaigama. Long story short, there was this reluctance, and more reluctance to aggressively train in counterinsurgency those men and women that the Nigerians wanted to.

I held a number of hearings on it. In one particular hearing we found out that 187 Nigerian units and 173 police units would be fully Leahy-vetted. They were clear and could be trained, and again I asked question after question about that. We had full committee hearings on it as well, all because we wanted the Nigerians who have a very capable military to have that very special training to take it to Boko Haram and defeat that insidious enemy. I am always wondering, you know, again, what the interface is with AFRICOM on that because I know when we would meet with the military people in Abuja they were gung-ho. They can take it to them and they can defeat them, and obviously Boko Haram got worse and worse by the year and stronger and stronger.

Secondly, on the issue of trafficking, in the year 2000 I wrote the Trafficking Victims Protection Act, our landmark law on combating trafficking. We wrote into it the standards that judge countries as to how poorly or well they are doing on combating trafficking, how well their militaries are doing. We contacted the Bush administration in 2001. He stood up a zero-tolerance policy. Combatant commanders are to have people, as you know so well, that work on trafficking.

And my question would be, and we have talked about this before, how is AFRICOM able to promote aggressively the idea of zero-tolerance in trafficking in the militaries of Africa?

It seems to be, you know, the peer to peer contact more than anybody at State or anybody in Congress could have a very effective impact on they taking up those best practices that the U.S. military has honed so well. General?

General WARD. Thank you, Congressman, and I will be brief as I respond to your two points here. Firstly, with respect to the reluctance of Nigeria to do what it did, on the one hand our association with the Nigerian military such that they are responding to their civilian authorities works. And therein lies, from my perspective, where the problem was, because the political environment prohibited the Nigerian military from doing all that those leaders and others that you indicated would certainly want to do.

It even had an impact on my ability to engage during my time as commander there in Nigeria because of a political environment that just restricted our presence and our involvement, so in my estimation that was the problem at that time. I am happy to say that that is no longer the case as it was and the level of interaction is enhanced and improving, and I believe that the training that we can offer, support, the training assistance, is in fact the training assistance that makes sense for them.

And therein lies into the second question with respect to trafficking. The more we are engaged and involved, our U.S. service members, be they sailors, soldiers, airmen, marines, are true Ambassadors for America. And when our young women and men are with the military and security forces of these other nations, they tend to adopt more or less our habits, if you will, and those are habits that respect the rights of individuals where those militaries have seen as protectors of their people across the gamut. And the issue of zero-tolerance in trafficking is seen as it is not something we do, we are here to protect our people as opposed to oppressing them and the more we are engaged, to include the programs like IMET, which is that long-term engagement, help to reinforce those ideals amongst the military members of our partner friends.

Mr. SMITH. Out of time, but thank you so very much, General. And thank you, all of you.

Chairman ROYCE. Thank you, Chairman Smith. We now go to Brad Sherman of California.

Mr. SHERMAN. Mr. Carroll, our economy is about seven times the size of France, yet they export 1½ dollars' worth of goods to Africa for each dollar we export. What are they doing or we are doing wrong, and in particular are our Embassies doing as much as they should to promote American exports? I would note that Germany even exports more to Africa than we do. France may have an advantage because of its prior colonial status. Germany has no such advantage. How do we export more?

Mr. CARROLL. Well, with reference to France, Mr. Congressman, you of course do mention that there are many historical relationships of a commercial nature. One thing that struck me about observing the French relationship with Africa at a commercial sense is they take it at a very, very high level even to the office of the President. There has been a historic relationship between the presidency and their former African colonies, and as you know the French system of corporations tends to run very closely along political lines. So there are many, many, shall we say, buttons to push that engage and enlarge that Franco-African relationship. I could talk a lot about that but I will just say that it is an historic one.

I think that we could do more at the Embassy level. I was certainly encouraged over the expansion of the U.S. Commerce Department's offices and presence in Africa, because I believe that these Foreign Commercial Service offices can really go out and identify not only market opportunities but also play a particularly strong role, Mr. Sherman, in assisting strong and medium enterprise U.S. companies that may not have——

Mr. SHERMAN. Mr. Carroll, I have to go on to another question.

Mr. CARROLL. Okay. Thank you, sir.

Mr. SHERMAN. It has just been my experience that foreign ministries of other countries put a lot more political pressure and effort into exports than our State Department.

And Ambassador, we are seeing a humanitarian disaster in South Sudan. Some of have suggested an arms embargo but that might just leave the Nuer at the tender mercies of President Kiir. Often when you can't create an atmosphere of peace you can at least create a balance of power and separation of warring parties. What can we do so that we don't see a slaughter of the Nuer people and that we restore peace to South Sudan?

Ambassador BRIGETY. Congressman, thank you for the question. First of all, as you know, very briefly, almost all of our normal interventions have failed, not only those of ourselves but also those of IGAD, the regional economic community, and others. And to be frank, the leaders of both the government and the opposition have become masters at manipulating the outside negotiators and they are not serious about peace nor are they, frankly, serious about the welfare of their own people.

In my view, Congressman, the leaders of South Sudan have lost their legitimacy and also lost their right to sovereignly govern their country. If ever there were a place in the world that were ripe for renewed U.N. trusteeship, it is South Sudan.

Mr. SHERMAN. That being the case, is this a matter of creating a balance of power between two forces led by evil men or is this something where we can't accomplish anything unless we can, we with our allies in Africa, can go in on the ground and restore order?

Ambassador BRIGETY. I believe that the current leadership of South Sudan must be replaced.

Mr. SHERMAN. Got you.

Ambassador BRIGETY. Preferably with indictments in front of the ICC. And——

Mr. SHERMAN. I would point out though that I don't see any country with the stomach to—it is one thing to indict in Europe at the ICC, it is another thing to serve those indictments on the leaders of the two sides in South Sudan and to compel their attendance and I don't know if the world has a willingness to send troops in to achieve that.

I have just a few more seconds and I want to make a point that not only do we see a terrible budget, as you indicated, but there is a complete failure to appoint anybody. As I understand it, we don't have any Assistant Secretary for Africa and we don't have an Acting Assistant Secretary for Africa, really, because the person we have filling that job doesn't have the qualifications, the technical legal qualifications to even be called acting assistant. Anything we can do to get some people over there?

Ambassador BRIGETY. We might ask the Trump administration to appoint someone yesterday because it is vital that we move quickly in this regard.

Mr. SHERMAN. Yes. And I point out these are not appointments pending in the Senate. These are appointments they just haven't gotten to, and if they just perhaps let the Secretary of State make these appointments we could go forward rather than having the White House personnel office deal with them. And I yield back.

Chairman ROYCE. We go now to Dana Rohrabacher of California.

Mr. ROHRABACHER. Thank you very much. And let me just note that our chairman has taken an interest in Africa since he came here. I remember I was surprised. We both come from Orange County, California, and I was surprised when he came here that he became so dedicated to making sure that Africans' needs were met and that we were paying attention to what was going on there. And he has been doing that for 20 years now, so there you go.

I would like to bring up an issue that perhaps it touches on everything we have been saying, but it is something that nobody seems to ever look at. We have here a situation where you have millions of people living, millions, tens of million, hundreds of millions of people living in abject poverty.

The level of human suffering as compared to other places on the planet is probably the worst, if not—probably the worst human suffering that is going on is in Africa. And yet, Africa is a continent that is so rich in resources. I mean it is—obviously there is a vast wealth associated with the fundamentals of resources in Africa, but yet hundreds of millions of people living desperate lives.

And I will have to say that it is not their fault obviously, it is the fault of a system, and what part of the system now, what we haven't really talked about and what people don't talk about is what I happen to believe is an important part of the system in a way, and without it all these maladies, the bad guys that are exploiting and causing this deprivation of so many people would not be able to succeed without this element, and here it is.

All of these things what you said, our friend from the National Geographic Society, Mr. Christy, your video showed all these guys with the ivory and such. Don't they have to have a bank to put that money into? Aren't these leaders, these various leaders in these countries and the various political people there, stealing money and putting it in Western banks?

Isn't the financial community in some way responsible when it takes billions of dollars of graft, of ivory money, and of money from people who are stealing it from these poor countries, the leaders of those countries? Aren't we talking about the global financial system here? What responsibility do they play in this? And that is my question for the whole panel. I would go first with our friend Christy because I mentioned him.

Mr. CHRISTY. Thank you very much, Congressman. For the worst groups, the most violent groups operating in Central Africa, they operate primarily on a barter system so they are trading ivory for arms. And in the case of the LRA and the Janjaweed, to the extent there is a money face to that, that is really going to Khartoum, Sudan, the Sudanese Government. But you are absolutely right.

Mr. ROHRABACHER. Right, but even if they are trading for arms, eventually somebody is paying for those arms, right?

Mr. CHRISTY. Right.

Mr. ROHRABACHER. I mean we are talking about a system here. And the system, I believe, ends up with billions of dollars in somebody's bank where they are able to use that money for whatever bankers use it for.

Mr. CHRISTY. As a criminal investigator I look for weak nodes. So I look for places where if you are moving product you have to bring it up in a port. You can take it out of a jungle, we can't find you there. You can sell it to a consumer in the Chinese market, we can't find you there. But we can find you at the port where it has to emerge.

And the financial system is a similar opportunity. You are putting your finger on financial crimes and the END Wildlife Trafficking Act gets to some of this appropriately. There is a financial aspect, a money laundering aspect, and it is worth exploring.

Mr. ROHRABACHER. Anybody else have a comment? I have 9 seconds left.

Well, Mr. Chairman, I would suggest, and I know this is a very delicate thing, but I think we need to have some focus in a hearing on the role that international financial institutions are playing in problems like this, because I believe the people of Africa are being robbed and their accomplices in this crime are Western banks.

Chairman ROYCE. I think, if the gentleman would yield?

Mr. ROHRABACHER. Yes.

Chairman ROYCE. I remember a conversation I had with a bank executive where I raised this issue in Europe about money that was held by Charles Taylor and I made the allegation that $30 million was held in that particular institution. And I remember this executive saying, "It is not $30 million, we have $23 million," which astounded me, but nevertheless we gave that information to the Treasury Department.

But it is certainly the case that if we could create more transparency, and I would say that this most applies to heads of state and to senior government officials, cabinet officials and so forth. If we had that kind of transparency out of the financial system where at a certain level that information became available, I think it would be a disincentive all over the world for those involved in bad governance.

At that point it is probably better if you are the head of state or an executive to go ahead and slap your name on a hospital and build that for your people rather than transfer it out of the country with the knowledge that that might be exposed and taken from you. It is probably a better legacy to at least spend it internally in the country.

And I think moving forward the gentleman raises a good point. We should work with the international community on a strategy that creates disincentives with respect to kleptocracy. We go now to Mr. Gregory Meeks of New York.

Mr. MEEKS. Thank you, Mr. Chairman. I want to agree with Mr. Rohrabacher on two things. One, what you are talking about with reference to the banks; but two, the extraordinary dedication and focus you have had, Mr. Chairman, as chairman of the subcommittee at one point and now as chairman of the committee. You have taken a number of us over to visit and you have had a real focus and attention on Africa and I want to thank you for that.

And of course the extraordinary contributions that the ranking member of the subcommittee has had on Africa. And, you know, and somebody mentioned two names that need to be mentioned anytime that I think of Africa, long before I came to Congress, I mean that is Congressman Charles Rangel and Congressman Donald Payne, Senior, and surely we miss them.

But I know and just want to make sure the extraordinary work that Congresswoman Bass has made, because we thought that it was going to be a huge vacuum when we lost them, but she has made sure that that has not happened and I want to thank her for her focus.

Let me also thank all of the panelists, particularly, well, all of you, but particularly to General Ward for your service to the United States of America and what you have done and the commitment that you have made to this country, and to Ambassador Brigety because I couldn't agree with you more. You know, when we look at the State Department it is tremendously important to our foreign affairs. And in fact I would say, for the military and the State Department, it is the balance of the scale that makes foreign policy work. With one without the other we are in deep—I won't say the word. But I just wanted to thank you so much for that.

So let me just ask two quick questions, one to Ambassador Brigety. I couldn't agree more with your opening statement. Maybe you could articulate the dangers of some of the programs that you think that would be devastated that are so important for our State Department with reference to working with Africa, and maybe you can articulate a few of those programs.

Ambassador BRIGETY. Thank you, Congressman. So the budget document that was submitted by the President says that there would be no decrease in funding for health and particularly for PEPFAR, neither would there be any decrease in humanitarian accounts.

So if one suggests that proposition, but then also suggests that there has to be some massive cuts somewhere if you want to achieve that objective there are two accounts that I am particularly worried about. The first is with regard to our democracy and governance accounts, particularly both of those accounts, per se, but also our economic support funds that can be used, broadly speaking, to support that.

The African continent, with 54 sovereign members that are recognized by the U.N., 55 when you include Western Sahara, could be the largest democratic region in the world both because of the number of countries there as well as because of the commitment to democracy in pan-African documents themselves.

But as the chairman noted, there are democracies under assault across the continent and if the United States does not step up to be a partner with pan-African institutions as well as national governments, there is not another major partner in the world that will be similarly positioned both in terms of resources it can apply and also in terms of its value set to continue to support the march toward democracy at a time when the Chinese and others are suggesting to other Africans elites that there is an alternative model for governance, namely, essentially, various forms of authoritarianism, which would be tragic.

The second thing I am really worried about is the Mandela Washington Fellowship Program, or YALI, which has been an incredible tool in the very short period of time it has existed, both to identify young African talent and also to find ways to encourage that young African talent to engage in their own countries and to teach them and to help expose them to means of Western governance, Western political engagement, and what not.

And I can promise you, in an environment where young Africans are looking for ways to fill their aspirations we want them to be looking toward us and not elsewhere.

Mr. MEEKS. Thank you. I also just want you to know that you must have been great at the State Department. I have had Madelina Young-Smith now with me for awhile and she is excellent too.

Mr. Carroll, I want to ask you a quick question. What investment opportunities that may be going unrealized for U.S. firms, what would you look at and say that there is other opportunities that we may be able to be taking advantage of but they are not currently taking advantage of?

Mr. CARROLL. Well, I will just mention two, sir, I think in the area of engineering and design services. I think the U.S. firms have an awful lot to offer and I think they are often in the second-tier firms that might have real strengths in providing those services to Africa. So I do think in the design and engineering and architectural field I think there are a lot of service opportunities in Africa.

But also in agribusiness, sir, I do believe that Africa is at a pivot. I think its future will be to have to modernize, to learn some of the lessons of the Green Revolution of India. And I think American agribusiness companies, particularly those that offer technologies such as irrigation systems, inputs of, you know, farm and herd management solutions, are going to find Africa to be a massive opportunity because Africa has the largest percentage of undeveloped, arable land in the entire globe.

Chairman ROYCE. We go now to Mike McCaul, Chairman Mike McCaul of Texas.

Mr. MCCAUL. Thank you, Mr. Chairman. I chair the Homeland Security Committee and one thing I have found time and time again is that terrorism thrives in failed states, in poverty, in safe havens. Unfortunately, Africa has many of those as we look at Boko Haram, Al Shabaab, al-Qaeda, and the Maghreb. And I think we have made some progress. The Millennium Challenge Corporation has been helpful. The Gates Foundation, I have met with Bill

Gates. The ONE Campaign is trying to move forward in this development of Africa.

My first question, General, is to you. I visited Camp North in the Sinai Peninsula where ISIS is prevalent, then went to Tunisia and visited with the Libyan team. Libya is still very much a strong threat to the homeland in terms of the numbers of ISIS, as is Sinai. General Haftar in the east, and then you have General al-Sarraj in Tripoli, it seems to me if the military can't get it together then you can't have governance, and if you can't have governance then you have terrorism.

Can you tell us where we are with that and what can we do more to foster a unified government in Libya?

General WARD. Thank you, Congressman McCaul. And obviously my understanding of it is from a position of afar, not directly involved these days. However, there are some things that I think are substantially important in moving along in these regions that you have described. To be sure, fragile states, failing states, are breeding grounds for nefarious activities of all sorts—human trafficking, narcotics trafficking—certainly terrorist havens for training and exporting that violence globally.

Where we as the United States of America are involved in a sustained way to, one, help security forces who are responsible for their territories be better prepared to do that makes a difference. Equally important is our engagement and from a developmental perspective to cause those who are living in those areas to see what I call this horizon of hope. Because where they are, there are things being done for them by their government, and by those who would support their attempts to have things provided from a literacy perspective, from a health perspective, that will help increase their ability to live the way that we as any human beings would want to live.

Mr. McCAUL. And I agree. But how do we get these two generals to work it out? I mean that seems to be the key problem in Libya to me.

General WARD. I would be happy to have a private conversation with you about that.

Mr. McCAUL. Okay. We have a SCIF in the Capitol.

General WARD. But the essence, sir, is causing their behavior to change, similar to what we see in South Sudan. And unless and until that happens, making progress will be very, very difficult, so causing their behavior to change so that they are less selfishly motivated and motivated for the good of the country opposed to not.

Mr. McCAUL. Thank you.

Mr. Christy, so terrorist financing, this is really quite horrific. They are using ivory to finance terrorism in Africa, and I commend what you have done to try to track this down. Can you tell us about the wildlife trafficking bill that this committee passed, how that is helping in this effort and what more can we do to shut that down. And we know that there is cocaine coming in from South America, you know, on the west coast of Africa to funnel in and finance this as well, but tell us about the impact of that legislation and what more we can do?

Mr. CHRISTY. Thank you, Congressman. I think, you know, all of this takes more time than we want. That bill, the law was signed,

I think, in October of '16, so it is really too early to tell the impact. Certainly identifying the countries is the next step, the problem countries as traffickers, and that has proved in the ivory world to be significant.

So to take it the next step and identify countries that are linked with extremist groups and the trafficking in these materials—ivory, rhino horn, et cetera—will be significant. The world needs diplomatic pressure on these countries to address these problems. These groups, I mean one of the things where we could make a big improvement is to look at the ways we have siloed these problems.

So we tend to look at wildlife trafficking as a wildlife problem and we think it is the aegis of biologists to address. We don't do that with cocaine. We don't put botanists in charge of the cocaine trafficking problem. If we move out of the biologist mindset and move to a law enforcement mindset, we begin to change how we think about these problems.

So as an example, I was in Garamba National Park which has been under siege from South Sudanese poachers, LRA, all these bad guys in this area, and I looked at the maps that they had for tracking the poaching groups and very detailed maps that they pin every day to update. And I had the opportunity to fly over to Central African Republic and spend time with the African Union forces there and I noticed they had similar maps and they overlapped and they had pins in those maps with different poacher and extremist group movements.

And I said do you guys talk to each other? No. And so I introduced them and they began talking and they had suspicions about the activities of the other. The park ranger suspected the Uganda military was poaching from helicopters. So two things happened, one, we were able to clear that up to their satisfaction; and two, they could begin exchanging intel. And that sort of intelligence sharing is critically important.

Mr. MCCAUL. I am well beyond my time. Thank you, Mr. Chairman.

Mr. CHRISTY. Sorry.

Chairman ROYCE. Thank you. We go now to Mr. David Cicilline of Rhode Island.

Mr. CICILLINE. Thank you, Mr. Chairman. I too want to thank you for your longtime commitment to Africa and the great leadership you have provided, and also acknowledge the extraordinary passionate and effective leadership of our ranking member of the subcommittee, Karen Bass, who has made her work in this area known not only throughout our country but throughout the region, and I really want to thank her for that.

General Ward, I want to ask you. There are currently nine U.N. peacekeeping missions deployed to various parts of the African continent constituting more than 82 percent of all U.N. peacekeepers serving in the field. Peacekeeping operations, as you know, are some of the most visible and consequential activities undertaken by the U.N. and play a very important role in advancing peace and security.

And I am interested, you know, given your experience as AFRICOM's commander, you know, what you would say in terms of the role of peacekeepers in terms of peace and security in Africa and particularly in your experience what makes some peacekeeping operations more successful than others and are there best practices that we should be analyzing and incorporating to future missions so that we can even enhance the effectiveness of peacekeeping missions further?

General WARD. Thank you, Congressman. Two critical elements to effective peacekeeping, one is obviously being resourced and trained appropriately in order to conduct a mission. The second has to do with the will of the government that provides the peacekeeping forces and how that is infused into the conduct of those peacekeeping forces as they execute their mission.

When you have those two—and obviously it is all underwritten by a mandate that allows what needs to be done to in fact be done. But if those forces are resourced and trained adequately and the government will to accomplish the mission is there, then peacekeeping forces are effective. And there were varying degrees of that that I witnessed across the continent.

I would also add, Congressman, while we are talking about that, peacekeeping in and of itself is one dimension of providing that stability and security. If it is not accompanied by a healthy dose of developmental support, such that the peacekeeping void if it is not filled can be filled by something that makes sense to the people, then that peacekeeping effort goes on and on and on, which we also see.

So peacekeeping in and of itself is one piece of it, one aspect of it, but the void, the requirements for development assistance, support, progress and that certainly has the underlying effect of governance as well so that those things support it, will, forces that are trained, resources are important.

Mr. CICILLINE. Thank you very much. That sort of gets to my next question and this is for you, Mr. Carroll. In recent years we have witnessed a narrowing of political space in countries like the Democratic Republic of Congo, Rwanda, Uganda, Burundi, and the Republic of the Congo. This has been coupled with efforts by many of these leaders to extend their tenures in power through constitutional coups which eliminate term limits for the incumbent.

What are the concrete measures the State Department and USAID should be taking to support democratic institutions and help reverse this worrying trend; and a related question, how should African leaders' amendment or circumvention of constitutional term limits impact U.S. bilateral aid in your judgment?

Mr. CARROLL. Well, I think we should continue to work with institutions in the countries that we can work with. They could include the media. They could include the legislative branch. They could include civil society organizations that we believe can bring domestic as well as external leverage, because I think it has to be not just us, we have to have domestic sources in the fight.

But from a business perspective, if you don't mind, Mr. Congressman, I find that unpredictability in the business environment is one of the greatest discouragements to foreign direct investment. And I think we in the business community and through perhaps our local counterparts and business associations need to carry that message that if you are going to want to do business with us, if you are going to want to attract technology and investment we need to have a measure of predictability in these countries. Congo is a perfect case in point, a country with vast mineral and agricultural potential that largely goes undeveloped because of this issue of unpredictability.

Mr. CICILLINE. Great, thank you so much.

I want to ask just one last question for you, Mr. Ambassador. One very concerning trend during political protests and elections in sub-Saharan Africa is that the governments have shut down access to the internet and other forms of communication in order to limit dissent. This has recently occurred in Ethiopia, Gabon, Cameroon, Uganda, and the Democratic Republic of the Congo, making it very difficult for citizens and journalists to report human rights violations or electoral irregularities.

I would be interested to know what actions you think our Government should take to mitigate this threat to the freedom of information and legitimate political expression in the sub-Saharan Africa.

Ambassador BRIGETY. Thank you, Congressman. Very briefly, the first obvious one is for robust engagement with those governments to demonstrate to them why it is crucially important, notwithstanding political differences, to continue to have open media space. Because at the end of the day, if people are not allowed to air their grievances peacefully they will do so forcefully, and I think that clearly is the lesson in Ethiopia, for example.

And then secondarily, depending on the situation there are obviously tools and techniques that are resident within USAID and also at civil affairs units to be able to make access to internet available on a sort of more regional or smaller scale basis. But even those things, as I said in my testimony, require resources and I think it is important to continue to fund those things.

Mr. CICILLINE. Thank you so much. And thank you, Mr. Chairman. I yield back.

Chairman ROYCE. Thank you. We go to Ted Yoho from Florida.

Mr. YOHO. Thank you, Mr. Chairman. And thank you, panel, for being here, very engaging and I really appreciate it. And I know a lot of the talk has focused on cutting foreign aid and I was one of those ones when I came up here 4 years ago to get rid of foreign aid, but I have become much more learned in my 4 years here.

And, you know, I realize and I agree with Secretary Mattis, who says if you cut foreign aid save that money and buy ammunition with it, and I truly believe that. But I bring that up because we are in a financial crisis in this country that is going to get worse if we don't deal with the underlying problem which is mandatory spending and we have to address those things. And if not, what you are seeing today is a sign. It is a tremor.

I got a report at the beginning of the year that said our seniors in Social Security were going to get a 25 percent cut across the board on Social Security checks within 12 years. And when it comes down to our seniors or foreign aid, you know where it is going to go. So I say that because you guys are the ones that need to make sure that our money on the ground is doing the work it is supposed to be doing.

And our goal, my goal is to transition all of our countries that we are giving foreign aid to, to go from a model of aid to trade, and that is why I am so excited about the OPIC models and the MCC. They have accountability. They have metrics in place. And as good as they are we need to make them better. If we look at our top 15 trading partners, 12 of those were recipients of foreign aids. I think South Korea is a great example and we can look at country after country that has done the same thing.

And so with that several questions came up. What is the major impediment in these developing countries to build out their infrastructure? We went to the Congo with Chairman Royce and Ranking Member Engel. And if you look at the whole continent of Africa it is approximately 1.11 billion people. This is the 21st century; 650 million people do not have electricity. And we were strong proponents of Electrify Africa, the Global Food Initiative, and the other bills that Chairman Royce spoke about. Six hundred and fifty million people don't have electricity.

And you look at the billions and billions of dollars this nation has invested of these people's monies out here and the trillions of dollars around the world, what is that major impediment that you see that prevents a country from taking care of their own people instead of taking care of the rulers? How do we change that too, so the impediment and what do you see?

Ambassador Brigety, if you would?

Ambassador BRIGETY. Congressman, thank you very much. Let me begin by saying that as a taxpayer myself of course I obviously believe very much in the effective stewardship of American taxpayer dollars and as with every program there are obviously ways in which they can continue to be refined and efficiencies found and things of that nature.

But at the same time one also has to make sure that we are making effective investments for not only for——

Mr. YOHO. Absolutely.

Ambassador BRIGETY [continuing]. The major of our security, but also for the growth of our partners. With regard to infrastructure investments, broadly speaking, I think it goes something to what my colleague Tony Carroll said which is, one, infrastructure are long term and big picture investments. And as one senior investor once told me, capital is cowardly. It does not want to go to places where there is substantial insecurity. So in this sense, the nature of good governance to ensure both a stable sort of peaceful environment as well as a stable regulatory environment is vital toward attracting the long term capital necessary to build infrastructure.

The second also is, frankly, having willing investors that are prepared to take risk, notwithstanding what I just said about insecurity, and the Chinese have proven that it can be done. The Ethiopians have proven that it can be done in terms of, you know, marshalling capital for the Grand Renaissance Ethiopian Dam. I am one who happens to believe that the future of Africa's next chapter of their history will be defined by private sector-led economic development.

And as somebody who is a diplomat who constantly thinks through foreign policy implications, I can also tell you that we simply cannot be able to maintain our position with partnership with the continent without the robust involvement of the American private sector and particularly as it relates to American——

Mr. YOHO. Well, and that is what I like about OPIC because they put the metrics and they will fund those organizations or the private sector. And if you look at 1961, the majority of the foreign investment in countries was foreign governments. Today that is only 9 percent. The rest is coming from the private sector.

And Mr. Carroll, you were talking about—oh, shoot. I forgot what I was going to say. You were talking about the investment with OPIC and how we can make that more effective in those countries. Can you expound just a little bit? I have only 4 seconds, so I guess you can't.

Mr. CARROLL. We have 2 seconds. I think we can do more leveraging with domestic capital. I think there are many pension funds and other institutions on a national and regional level that OPIC could do more work for and do a little bit more leveraging. We can have a separate discussion or I can respond to other questions in a longer discussion.

Mr. YOHO. Great, thank you. Appreciate your time, thank you all.

Chairman ROYCE. We go now to Dr. Ami Bera of California.

Mr. BERA. Thank you, Mr. Chairman. And I will echo the statements of many of my colleagues in the leadership that the chairman of the full committee and certainly the leadership of the ranking member of the Subcommittee on Africa and Human Rights has shown.

This morning I had the opportunity to address the Meridian International Center's global dialogue with African women leaders and in the conversation that we had, the importance of recognizing the global interconnectedness that you know, we can no longer think of ourselves as isolated.

I look at this from the perspective as a physician. You have public health crises that occur in Africa, they clearly matter to what happens here in the United States. From that public health perspective you don't wait until it hits our shores, you make those investments and you go to the epicenter and address that. So, I was listening to my colleague Mr. Yoho's comments and I agree with them that we have to be fiscally sound and make sure we are making the right investments, but the return on investments are also incredibly important.

In that sense, when we think about our three planks of our foreign policy, it has three legs on it. Not just defense, but it has diplomacy and development. And that development component often is overlooked because, yes, you might be spending $1 today, but what you are doing is potentially avoiding $10 in defense costs or public health costs, or the tolls. How do you put a price on a human life? So, I applaud President Bush and his initiatives, and PEPFAR had huge returns, huge returns on the saving of life.

Ambassador Brigety, you served in the State Department during the 2011 famine in East Africa and also as our representative to the African Union during the 2013 Ebola crisis. You have touched on how this is not the time for the United States to change its priorities and withdraw from a region, and I would be curious knowing that we are facing another potentially devastating crisis and famine and loss of life in the coming years what would you advise us at this juncture?

Ambassador BRIGETY. Well, Congressman, thank you very much for the thoughtful question. There is both I think, an obvious and then a less obvious answer. The obvious answer is that we clearly need to be continuing to support our health accounts and our humanitarian assistance accounts for the sorts of interventions that were necessary, for example, to respond to the 2011 famine in Somalia as well as the 2014 Ebola crisis.

But the less obvious component is that there are profound diplomatic interventions that make that kind of response possible. Let me give you an example. During the 2014 Ebola crisis I lost years off my life in helping to respond to that crisis because by the summer of 2014 we were seriously looking at epidemiological curves that would say we would have 1 million dead Africans within 6 months, by January, unless we were able to flood the zone of Liberia, Guinea, Conakry, and Sierra Leone with healthcare workers to actually respond to the crisis.

So we did a lot of behind the scenes diplomatic work to get the African Union in the fight so that by December of that year they had nearly 1,000 healthcare workers from across the continent that converged on those three countries to provide direct patient support to people that were affected. Now the Africans deserve enormous credit for stepping up, but frankly it would have taken at a minimum a lot longer to do so had we not done a lot of depth diplomacy behind the scenes that nobody ever saw.

And we are already at the next time with regard to Ebola in the DRC and as to regards to the three unfolding famines on the continent, which is why it so critical for us to be able to maintain that capability to develop the kind of trust that is necessary with our African partners so we can respond to these crises.

Mr. BERA. Wonderful. I think of America as a great nation, but it is also that idea of America, those values that we represent. And a great nation—when they see famine and when they see public health crisis—doesn't retreat from the world, a great nation leads with our moral values. We see the humanitarian crisis. We see the public health crisis and we lead. And it is that idea of America that we have to hold onto. That idea of American leadership that for generations folks have believed in.

As I listened to these African women leaders, that is what their worry is that yes, we have domestic challenges here, but you know what, it is that idea of who we are as a nation, that greatness we can't let that disappear. Thank you and I will yield back.

Chairman ROYCE. We go now to Dan Donovan of New York.

Mr. DONOVAN. Thank you, Mr. Chairman. I apologize for my tardiness, I had another matter, but some of these questions may have been asked already. I am a member of the subcommittee that deals with Africa and global health of our larger committee. And maybe because 2 weeks after I was elected to this office, at 58 years old, I had my very first baby—her mother actually calls her my very last baby—but I got this great interest. I am honored to serve on this committee that deals with global health about women and children who are dying from preventable diseases, things that we have vaccinations for that for some reason or another are either unavailable or we can't get to mothers and babies who are suffering in African countries. I understand we have gotten better at it over the years, but there still seems to be some obstacles.

And I don't know who the proper person on the panel is to answer this question, but if somebody could just give me some insight on how successful you feel we have been and what we could do to be even further along in our success in helping mothers and babies in Africa.

Mr. CARROLL. If I might jump in here because I have done a fair amount of work with the Gates Foundation—polio in Nigeria—and continue to do a lot of work with Merck, the world's largest vaccine company and their projects in Africa. I think it can't happen without building the health infrastructure in these countries. Many of these countries spend $4 to $6 per person per year on their health. Without developing a fulsome health infrastructure, any vaccination campaign, any type of preventive mechanism will not be successful, and it has to be led from leaders within that country, not just an externally-led foreign assistance program.

But I think it can happen. Certainly the success in polio eradication in Nigeria is an ongoing battle, but they have achieved a lot of success. In Rwanda they instituted an HPV vaccine program in Rwanda that produced incredible adherence among Rwandan women. I believe that cervical cancer is among the two largest killers of women in Africa and the only magic bullet we have in the world of vaccines is the HPV vaccine, which is extremely effective. They made a commitment to build out their infrastructure. They made a commitment from the top down that this is an important program.

So we have to engage leadership in getting the message. We have to help them build the infrastructure to staff and implement these programs. And we are not going to get it done if we are cutting the Fogarty Center and other CDC programs that are absolutely linchpins to these programs in Africa. We have to be able to be at their side, but it still has to be led from those countries. So thank you for that opportunity.

Ambassador BRIGETY. Congressman, if I may add to that and I am grateful for your passion on this issue. The issue with regard to building healthcare infrastructure in Africa is that it is not like building a bridge. I mean once it is built it is done and you can walk away. They are more like sort of living organisms in the sense that you have to continue to train new healthcare workers, one has to continue to deal with access and extension services in the rural areas or what not.

And this is why it is critically important for the United States to be able to maintain its capacity to help develop the long term infrastructure of healthcare systems in African countries. The Ebola crisis, I think, is very instructive in this regard. So we had been involved for many years in helping to develop the healthcare infrastructure in Liberia, for example, which is focused not only on primary care but also in helping to address HIV/AIDS.

With the advent of the Ebola crisis and its coming to Monrovia, the healthcare system in Liberia was devastated, and by that we mean doctors, nurses, in which we had invested many years, died and were no longer there. So the ability for us to continue to help train and educate and provide more and more healthcare officials not only is something that has to be sustained over time, but sus-taining it is clearly in our own national interest in addition to what it does for, you know, mothers and children in those countries. Be-cause the next time there is another major pandemic on the con-tinent we can't just insert a healthcare infrastructure, one has to develop it over time.

Mr. DONOVAN. Mr. Ambassador, could you—I don't know what some of the questions—do we find that the governments in the Af-rican countries are cooperative as well or are there people, are there regimes and governments that are trying to prevent their citizens from receiving the aid that we are so willing to provide?

Ambassador BRIGETY. Congressman, I am not aware of any Afri-can country that is not willing to partner on matters of health. In most places it is a matter of resources, to be frank, and it also may be a matter of a prioritization of those resources. So it might be, for example, the decision of whether or not you concentrate health services in the capital city versus extension services in rural areas, or focusing more on primary care as opposed to care for tertiary diseases like diabetes or cancer or other sorts of things.

General WARD. Mr. Donovan, a quick postscript if I might, Mr. Chair. Healthcare facilities on the continent of Africa are not the Walter Reed National Military Center of Bethesda. A quick exam-ple, in Comoros, where the USAID had a program where they were training local medical providers, we were able to partner with our USAID counterparts and using Department of Defense engineers, build a concrete block structure whereby medical practice could be accomplished. And providing clean water to that facility facilitated the provision of a health service that community did not have pre-viously and changed the whole dynamic in that community.

And these are the things that this 1 percent of our national budget that goes to promoting our international systems abroad. It creates feelings, creates a sentiment, creates the result that pays dividends on and on and on and helps to stabilize those environ-ments.

Mr. DONOVAN. That is a great example of our successes.

The last thing I just want because my time is way over as well, my colleague was talking about investment in Africa, private in-vestment. I met with a group, and my staff can supply you with their information, yesterday, called Rendezvous, who are devel-oping planned communities in seven African countries, so I would just offer that to you if you would like to hear more about it.

Thank you. Mr. Chairman, I yield whatever time I have left.

Chairman ROYCE. Thank you, Mr. Donovan. We go to Norma Torres from California.

Ms. TORRES. Thank you, Mr. Chairman, and thank you to our guest panelists here today. General Ward, in your testimony you made a very compelling case for why U.S. engagement in Africa is in our national interest and I very much agree with you on that.

Ambassador Brigety, you have also made a point and I want to share with you that the point that you have made on the Ebola cri-sis, you know, this point was driven home for many of our constitu-ents during the Ebola crisis in 2014 and 2015. We have had a real-ly great conversation here. I am new to the committee and I am trying to wrap my hands around all of these issues we have talked about, ivory being used to finance terrorism and these civil wars.

The one thing that we have not talked about, unfortunately, is how rape is being used also against women, against very young women in this continent. Projected U.S. global health funding for 2017 is an estimated $9.5 billion, all of which is subject to President Trump's Global Gag Rule, so let's talk about that for a little bit.

Every year, despite increased access to safe abortion procedures, 6 million African women end their pregnancies unsafely and 1.6 million are treated for complications. So when we talk about safety and we talk about saving, you know, these wonderful animals, what are we doing to help our young women in Africa and how are we helping to ensure that there is a healthcare system in place to help them get the necessary procedures that they need, whether that is family planning or what are we doing to teach them how to protect themselves from these abusers?

Ambassador BRIGETY. Congresswoman, thank you very much for that very important question. Both as a Deputy Assistant Secretary and also as an Ambassador I could spend days telling you about stories that I have encountered meeting women who are rape victims in Eastern Congo, refugee women in northern Kenya, et cetera, that have experienced exceptional trauma. And I have been very proud of the types of assistance that the United States has provided over time to address rape as a war crime, to provide services to help rape victims recover from these challenges.

With regard to your question about the Global Gag Rule let me say, Congresswoman, that I understand that the question of abortion is an incredibly sensitive one with deep feelings on both sides of the debate, one that we will not resolve here. But one thing that is absolutely accurate is that the nature of the Global Gag Rule as articulated and its expansion under the Trump administration will have negative, harsh, unintended consequences for women who desperately need gynecological care.

And it seems to me that if one is morally motivated with regard to the protection of life and compassion for those that are suffering, one would try at a minimum to find a way as you address these incredibly challenging moral questions that one does not harm those women that are desperately in need of the kinds of services that we provide.

Ms. TORRES. They are victims in two separate ways.

Mr. CHRISTY. May I add?

Ms. TORRES. Please.

Mr. CHRISTY. So one of the things that I was excited about bringing to the fore today was that when we are talking about these wildlife crime issues there is an opportunity to leverage that to do something more important or bigger. These rangers are on the ground in rural and remote areas and they represent the only law and order in those areas. In many of the worst areas in terms of violence these rangers are part of a public-private partnership. African Parks is one organization that brings together very disciplined guys to work with the local wildlife authorities to bring order, and the villagers in these places said to me they are my protector.

And some of the most dangerous forces in these remote areas are military, U.N. workers, as we know, and to have these smaller groups that are trained specifically and are working with Americans in many circumstances, you have an opportunity to address that.

Ms. TORRES. My time has expired.

General Ward, I hope to be able to have a conversation with you outside of these four walls. I think there is so much work to continue to do and I am really happy to help in any way that I can, Congresswoman Bass. The bigger humanitarian crisis that I am interested in helping in the region is how these policies are impacting women that have been raped, their children, who is taking care of them, and the LBGT community is another issue that we have not addressed here today, so I yield back my expired time.

Chairman ROYCE. Okay. Let's go to Lois Frankel of Florida.

Ms. FRANKEL. Thank you, Mr. Chair. Thank you, Ms. Bass. And thank you to the witnesses. As a member of this committee I have had an opportunity to be in Africa a number of times, different countries. I left this meeting. We have so many meetings going on at the same time, but the reason I left the meeting a few minutes ago was to meet with a group of African women who are in a leadership program. Many of them are in Parliament in different areas of Africa. They are just a lot of different, wonderful leaders, so that is where I was.

So it was interesting, because I wanted to ask them about a topic that Representative Torres brought up which is important not only to them, but I think to women all over the world and that is being able to be in control of your own body and to decide if and when you want to have a family because there is nothing that changes your life like having a family, right. I think everybody who has had a child knows that.

What I think is also important and I learned this—I was in Malawi last year in one of the villages and one of the things they were stressing was the need to get women into the economy. And that seems to be another worldwide issue—when you get women into the economy, you can double your productivity.

It is very, very hard, difficult, sometimes impossible for women to become part of the economy and to sustain themselves in an economy if they cannot be in control of their own ability to plan their family, so it is why this Global Gag Rule that President Trump has brought back is very, very worrisome. I know Representative Torres asked you about that.

And I just, I talked to these women just a few minutes ago and the word that I got back from them was cruel, it is cruel. Part of the cruelty is not just what it could potentially do to a woman's health, because this is just not all about abortion but this gag rule is a chilling effect to any healthcare provider who may use their own money to either perform an abortion or save a woman who has gone and had an illegal abortion which is apparently very prominent in Africa, so you have this chilling effect.

And what they said is, you know, if you are going to do this, which they of course they say, you know, why are you doing this, why don't you give us enough notice so that there is not a gap in services? But what I would like—I know you have commented with

Representative Torres on this issue. What I would like for you two is talk about, if you can, the importance of women's involvement in the economy and how important it is to keep them healthy and vibrant.

Mr. CARROLL. Let me just offer an observation on the economic inclusion of women. There are many societies that have de facto and de jure constraints about women owning a title to land, being able to establish a business, their of course being able to obtain business licenses, getting the training necessary. I think there is certainly a trend among these organizations such as those that you have met today to try to level the playing field so that women can play a more formal role in their economies. So I think this is a process that people have their eye on.

I won't comment on the gag order because I know there are people here that can talk at greater depth about that than I am, but I do think this idea of women inclusiveness in the economy is an issue that is being worked on.

General WARD. Congresswoman Frankel, I was in Africa last year, I believe, with the U.S. Global Leadership Coalition where we had a chance to visit with various activities that had some sponsorship put on that was part of our U.S. foreign assistance. In particular, we visited a farm that was owned by a woman and she and her children were doing things that were beyond any scope that that program had been designed to take care of, making huge, huge progress, but not just for her and her family.

She had also gathered and had caused other women to be a part of that co-op, if you will, creating a dynamic in that community that led to stability because their sons weren't being turned into terrorists. It led to increased health because they were producing products that were good for increasing their overall local health and the products were of such quality that they are being exported, bringing revenue into that community. Women—when they are allowed and empowered through health or through sponsorship and promotion to be entrepreneurs—definitely make a difference, a positive difference.

Ms. FRANKEL. Thank you. Thank you very much, and I yield back.

Chairman ROYCE. Thank you. And I would just note that Congresswoman Lois Frankel kept with the goal which was yielding back time when there is time still to yield back.

We go now to Ted—it still sets a new record. We now go to Ted Deutch of Florida.

Mr. DEUTCH. I thank you, Mr. Chairman. Mr. Chairman, there is strong bipartisan support in Congress for expanding our assistance to Africa and I know that we will put up a fight when the administration tries to cut U.S. support there in its 2018 budget. What worries me in the short term is the damage the President and his team have already done to our relationships with African leaders.

Secretary Tillerson invited the chair of the African Union to visit Washington and then blew him off. All 60 African leaders who were invited to an African trade conference in California had their visas denied by Trump's State Department, and the same State Department has no appointees to run offices and bureaus that oversee our work in Africa. We know the President wants to shutter one third of USAID's 100 missions and cut 30 percent of its budget, which would certainly mean cuts in Africa where the agency does the largest share of its work.

The signal from the Trump administration seems to be pretty clear that the United States doesn't respect African leaders, doesn't want to do the work of partnering with African nations, and doesn't value U.S. engagement on the continent. Now in Africa, every inch that we withdraw, countries like China are ready to step in, in ways that are damaging to U.S. interests and the long term well-being of the people of Africa.

Now Ambassador Brigety, I ask whether you worry that even before we begin this budget debate whether serious damage has already been done to our relationships with partners and friends in Africa, and also what is at stake if we abandon America's tradition of engagement and partnership with Africa in favor of what appears to be a rather incoherent and short-sighted withdrawal from Africa?

Ambassador BRIGETY. Congressman, thank you very much for the question. I just 2 weeks ago attended the World Economic Forum Africa in Durban, South Africa, and what I can tell you is in any number of conversations I had on the margins of that meeting with African business people, elected officials and what not, there is profound concern about the continued nature of American engagement in Africa under the Trump administration for reasons that you just articulated. I think that the way in which Chairperson Faki was treated was seen incredibly negatively not only by the African Union Commission but by African leaders across the continent. It is worth noting that to his great credit Secretary Tillerson subsequently had a phone call with Chairman Faki on May 8th to invite the chairperson to Washington, DC, for the next round of the U.S.-Africa strategic dialogue. One hopes that happens and that one can make up for those mistakes.

But as an outsider looking in that mistake and the mistake, for example, Rwandan President Paul Kagame, who is one of the most prominent leaders on the continent, was here in Washington about a little over a month ago, nobody from the administration met with him, neither anyone from the White House nor anyone in the State Department.

And this suggests either one of two things, either this administration has decided that Africa is not a strategic priority and that is what explains these various sorts of things, or what I believe is a more likely explanation is that the absence of senior leadership in the White House or at the State Department that is focused on Africa has helped abet at making what I think are, quite frankly, rookie mistakes with regard to engagement with the continent. And this is why I think it is so vital for the administration to move with alacrity to appoint senior people at the State Department, in the White House, and also at senior ambassadorships across the continent.

Mr. DEUTCH. I thank you, Ambassador. If you are right and we can chock this up to rookie mistakes as we wait for them to figure it out, as we wait for these positions to be filled, General Ward, what impact does that have from a national security standpoint and on U.S. forces?

General WARD. Congressman, we have to continue to cause our presence and our interests to be felt and realized in other areas until that day, then, does come. And so therefore we are not going to wring our hands, we are going to just reinforce our efforts in other areas. For example, next month the U.S.-Africa Business Summit will be here in DC hosted by the Corporate Council on Africa and certain African leaders will be in attendance.

And how support is rallied around to show that in spite of whatever else may be going on, there is still support for the continent and we do it through those sorts of programs and showing support, participating in and endorsing in ways that then as they return, based on a relationship that was established here, the word will be spread that it is not over and we have to just double down on our efforts to cause that to be the case.

Mr. DEUTCH. I appreciate that. Thanks to all the witnesses for being here today.

Chairman ROYCE. Would the gentleman yield just on a point?

Mr. DEUTCH. Of course.

Chairman ROYCE. Because I think we are in concurrence on a lot of issues, but I just wanted to address this issue of President Paul Kagame, because to bring this up without explaining that one of the reasons we did not on this committee ask for meetings with President Paul Kagame was because of several assassinations of political opponents outside his own country in a third country. On top of that we had the problem with his suppression of freedom of expression and the human rights abuses.

So once you have situations where you have assassinations, admitted assassinations, I think we could argue the point, but certainly that point was defended, you could understand why we weren't anxious to orchestrate a meeting while he was here in the first months of the new administration. So I think sometimes disclosing all of the factors in a situation like that would be important. That said, I want to thank our witnesses here today.

Mr. DEUTCH. Mr. Chairman.

Chairman ROYCE. Yes.

Mr. DEUTCH. Just before I yield back, I appreciate what you said. I would just add though that if we have a valid concern, if what is driving decisions like that is suppression of freedom of expression and concern about human rights, I would respectfully suggest that the President of the United States had no business meeting and welcoming President Erdogan to the White House. But I yield back.

Chairman ROYCE. Listen. Yes, I think—and you will see my statements on that point as well. But what I am trying to point out, I am trying to establish some objectivity when it comes to this debate because many of the points that we are raising here are points that we need to raise as a committee, but at the same time we have to be objective in terms of our choice of examples and not mislead.

And I think it is clear that as we are discussing the challenges that we want to see met in Africa, and there are many of the challenges that we have discussed here—the fact that some governments are kleptocratic in nature, the weak institutions that we spoke to, the Islamist extremists that are a problem for many governments, the wildlife trafficking and the way that that feeds into terror as well as the elimination, potentially, of the populations of elephants and certainly of the rhinoceros. I mean the very well likelihood that in our lifetime the rhinoceros will be an extinguished species if we don't turn this around.

And all of that draws people, if we can get sustainable development, draws people to see that magnificent continent and it supports the people in that continent, but there are also these tremendous opportunities. There is that great resource that Africa has which is the people of Africa. And the young people that I have had the opportunity to meet over many years of travel to the region in which our panel are all too familiar with, they want a better future. They want it and I believe that they will get it.

I believe it will help if we can work in a bipartisan way here to make sure that they get it. I think the United States has a stake in their future. I think supporting the growth of healthier, more stable communities in Africa serves our diplomatic, our economic, our humanitarian, and our security interests.

I think U.S. engagement can help prevent the spread of diseases. One of the issues is Ebola where this crosses borders and, frankly, can cross our own border. It can help prevent and address insecurity before extremism takes hold on these young minds, and it can help open new markets that will create opportunities for Americans as well as help communities in Africa grow their own way out of poverty.

So U.S. engagement with Africa is smart and essential, and I look forward to working with the administration and my colleagues here in Congress to ensure that we get this right.

And I thank again our panel. We are adjourned.

[Whereupon, at 12:12 p.m., the committee was adjourned.]

APPENDIX

FULL COMMITTEE HEARING NOTICE
COMMITTEE ON FOREIGN AFFAIRS
U.S. HOUSE OF REPRESENTATIVES
WASHINGTON, DC 20515-6128

Edward R. Royce (R-CA), Chairman

May 18, 2017

TO: MEMBERS OF THE COMMITTEE ON FOREIGN AFFAIRS

You are respectfully requested to attend an OPEN hearing of the Committee on Foreign Affairs, to be held in Room 2172 of the Rayburn House Office Building (and available live on the Committee website at http://www.ForeignAffairs.house.gov):

DATE: Thursday, May 18, 2017

TIME: 10:00 a.m.

SUBJECT: U.S. Interests in Africa

WITNESSES: General William E. Ward, USA, Retired
President and Chief Operating Officer
SENTEL Corporation
(Former Commander, U.S. Africa Command)

Mr. Bryan Christy
Explorer and Investigative Reporter
National Geographic Society

Mr. Anthony Carroll
Adjunct Professor
School of Advanced International Studies
Johns Hopkins University

The Honorable Reuben E. Brigety II
Dean
Elliott School of International Affairs
The George Washington University
(Former U.S. Representative to the African Union, U.S. Department of State)

By Direction of the Chairman

COMMITTEE ON FOREIGN AFFAIRS
MINUTES OF FULL COMMITTEE HEARING

Day __*Thursday*__ Date __*5/18/2017*__ Room __*2172*__

Starting Time __*10:10*__ Ending Time __*12:12*__

Recesses __*0*__ (___ to ___) (___ to ___) (___ to ___) (___ to ___) (___ to ___) (___ to ___)

Presiding Member(s)
Chairman Edward R. Royce

Check all of the following that apply:

Open Session ☑   Electronically Recorded (taped) ☑
Executive (closed) Session ☐   Stenographic Record ☑
Televised ☑

TITLE OF HEARING:
U.S. Interests in Africa

COMMITTEE MEMBERS PRESENT:
See attached.

NON-COMMITTEE MEMBERS PRESENT:
none

HEARING WITNESSES: Same as meeting notice attached? Yes ☑ No ☐
(If "no", please list below and include title, agency, department, or organization.)

STATEMENTS FOR THE RECORD: *(List any statements submitted for the record.)*
IFR - Rep. Dan Donovan
SFR - Rep. Gerald Connolly

TIME SCHEDULED TO RECONVENE __________
or
TIME ADJOURNED *12:12*

____
Full Committee Hearing Coordinator

HOUSE COMMITTEE ON FOREIGN AFFAIRS
FULL COMMITTEE HEARING

PRESENT	MEMBER	PRESENT	MEMBER
X	Edward R. Royce, CA	X	Eliot L. Engel, NY
X	Christopher H. Smith, NJ	X	Brad Sherman, CA
	Ileana Ros-Lehtinen, FL		Gregory W. Meeks, NY
X	Dana Rohrabacher, CA		Albio Sires, NJ
X	Steve Chabot, OH	X	Gerald E. Connolly, VA
	Joe Wilson, SC	X	Theodore E. Deutch, FL
X	Michael T. McCaul, TX	X	Karen Bass, CA
	Ted Poe, TX		William Keating, MA
	Darrell Issa, CA	X	David Cicilline, RI
	Tom Marino, PA	X	Ami Bera, CA
X	Jeff Duncan, SC	X	Lois Frankel, FL
X	Mo Brooks, AL	X	Tulsi Gabbard, HI
	Paul Cook, CA	X	Joaquin Castro, TX
X	Scott Perry, PA	X	Robin Kelly, IL
	Ron DeSantis, FL		Brendan Boyle, PA
	Mark Meadows, NC		Dina Titus, NV
X	Ted Yoho, FL	X	Norma Torres, CA
X	Adam Kinzinger, IL	X	Brad Schneider, IL
X	Lee Zeldin, NY		Tom Suozzi, NY
X	Dan Donovan, NY	X	Adriano Espaillat, NY
X	James F. Sensenbrenner, Jr., WI	X	Ted Lieu, CA
X	Ann Wagner, MO		
	Brian J. Mast, FL		
X	Brian K. Fitzpatrick, PA		
	Francis Rooney, FL		
X	Thomas A. Garrett, Jr., VA		

Strong Coffee, Stronger Women

Bill Gates
May 9, 2017
Of all the charts I've seen, this one is the most beautiful:

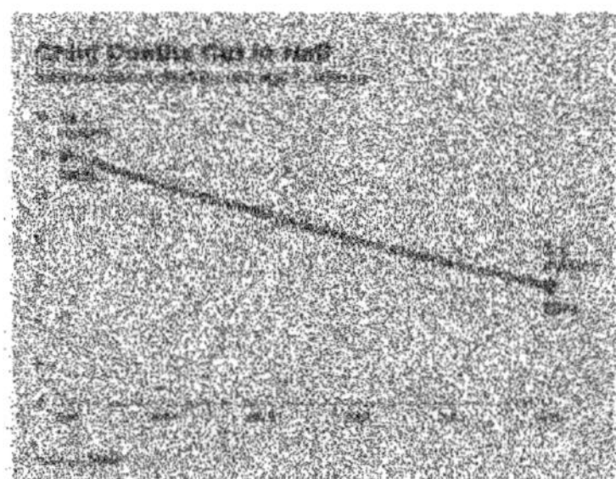

Why?

First, that descending red line captures one of the most amazing stories of human progress: It shows how the number of deaths of children under 5 per year has been cut in half since 1990.

Second, hidden along that line are millions of stories of the incredible work being done by heath officials, governments, donors, and parents around the world to help save all those lives.

Here's one of those stories. It begins with some remarkable women I met in Ethiopia. They are part of an innovative program that's improved the health of millions of children in their country.

Back in 1990, Ethiopia had one of the highest rates of child mortality in the world. One in five children were dying before their 5th birthdays. With few doctors and most of its population living in rural areas, Ethiopia struggled to provide basic health services to the country. Most women in rural areas gave birth at home.

Then in 2000, the Ethiopian government made a commitment to improve its healthcare system. Ethiopia signed on to the United Nations' Millennium Development Goals, which focused the world's attention on fighting disease and ending poverty by using data to measure progress on health and development progress. As part of the goals, Ethiopia pledged to reduce under-five death rates by at least two-thirds by 2015.

To achieve it, Ethiopia needed to find an effective way to deliver healthcare to the remotest corners of the country. But training thousands of new doctors to staff them would take years and would be extremely costly. Instead, Ethiopia created a community health worker program. They selected thousands of people, primarily young women with at least a 10th grade education, and trained them in a set of basic health skills—including how to deliver babies, administer immunizations, and provide family planning support—that are proven to save lives. Most of the health workers were recruited from the communities they served, helping to quickly build public trust in the new effort.

In 2012, I made my first trip to Ethiopia to see the program in action for myself. I was amazed. I visited a remote health post south of Addis Ababa run by two health workers, Yetagesu Alemu and Betula Shemesie. They spent many of their days walking from door to door in their village caring for pregnant women and families with newborns. Their health post didn't have electricity or any high tech medical equipment. Still, their efforts had made an impact on the health of the families in their community.

What was exciting to see was how this success was being repeated in villages across the country. Despite being one of the poorest countries in the world, Ethiopia managed to dramatically reduce the rate of child mortality. By 2012, Ethiopia had met the target for the Millennium Development Goal on child survival, with under-five death rates dropping by 66 percent since 1990.

One of the key reasons the program has been so effective is that the health workers are dedicated to measuring their progress. Covering nearly every square inch of the walls of the health post I visited were large charts, where the health workers would track births, immunizations, malaria cases, and other indicators. Each indicator helped them understand how well they were performing and which areas demanded more attention.

Today, Ethiopia has more than 15,000 health posts delivering primary health care to the farthest reaches of this rural country of 100 million people. The health posts are staffed by 38,000 health workers like Betula and Yetagesu.

Last summer, I had a chance to visit Ethiopia again. I caught up with Yetagesu and Betula over coffee and to learn more about how the health worker program was going. They told me how women who once delivered their babies at home were now choosing to give birth at health centers. Their communities also had access to ambulances that would pick up any woman who is ready to give birth. Yetagesu and Betula were also proud to report that they had received additional medical training to sharpen their health skills.

To be sure, there's a lot more work to be done to improve health services in rural Ethiopia. Their communities need more ambulances. Just one vehicle serves 17 health posts, Yetagesu said. They also hoped the country would hire more health workers so they would have the time to provide families with more comprehensive services. And as Melinda and I discussed in this year's annual letter, one of the biggest challenge in child survival is newborn deaths. In Ethiopia, about 44 percent of all childhood deaths occur within the first 28 days of life. We need to find innovative ways to solve this challenge.

Still, I'm confident that Ethiopia will continue to make progress in child survival. And what's most exciting is that Ethiopia's health program has been so successful that it now serves as a model for other countries to follow. Sharing lifesaving innovations like Ethiopia's ensures that in the years ahead the most beautiful chart in the world will become even more beautiful.

Statement for the Record
Submitted by Mr. Connolly of Virginia

It is impossible to convey accurately the breadth and depth of U.S. interests in Africa in one hearing. The world's second-largest and second-most populous continent has a wealth of diversity – with abundant natural resources; wildlife roaming its deserts, tropical jungles, and grasslands; and more than one billion people, from 3,000 ethnic groups, speaking 2,000 languages, in 54 nations. Suffice it to say, the United States has significant security, economic, and humanitarian interests in Africa, and protecting these interests requires each of the pillars of our foreign policy toolbox, namely diplomacy, development, and defense. However, the Trump Administration's wholesale retreat from U.S. global leadership and early policies toward Africa threaten to neglect current opportunities and undermine decades of U.S. investment. From Cape Town to Cairo, one consistent truth is that U.S. engagement is key.

Despite the monolithic narrative of "war, poverty, and disease," most African countries have progressed exponentially since independence from European colonial powers in the mid-20th century. Governments in Senegal, Ghana, South Africa, Botswana, and Namibia have developed into mature democracies with peaceful transfers of power and robust institutions. Six of the top thirteen countries with the highest compounded annual growth rate from 2014-2017 are located in Africa. The continent is home to the fastest growing population of consumers and entrepreneurial youth in the world. Approximately 60 percent of the sub-Saharan African population is under the age of 25. Declining birth and death rates are creating a window of opportunity for accelerated economic growth known as the demographic dividend.

These conditions present an enormous opportunity not only for many African economies, but also for U.S. businesses. However, certain social and economic policies are necessary to realize such gains and concerns about systemic corruption, poor governance, and infrastructure gaps have impeded U.S. private investment. That is why U.S. programs that promote the rule of law, good governance, and access to electricity are so critical. Last year, we enacted the Electrify Africa Act (P.L. 114-121), which aims to provide electricity to 50 million people and add 20,000 megawatts of electricity production by 2020. USAID estimates that these efforts will result in at least $100 million in power sector sales for export, leading to approximately 40,000 U.S. jobs by 2030.

The U.S. President's Emergency Plan for AIDS Relief (PEPFAR) is currently supporting lifesaving antiretroviral treatment for nearly 10 million men, women, and children in Africa. Since 2000, the President's Malaria Initiative has helped to save an estimated 6.8 million lives through the procurement and distribution of insecticide-treated mosquito nets and antimalarial treatments. With USAID's support to combat childhood illnesses and malnutrition, Ethiopia was able to reduce its child mortality rate by 67 percent from 1990 to 2013. Thanks to sustained U.S. investment in critical health interventions, the United States is poised to help end preventable child and maternal deaths worldwide within a generation. However, the Trump Administration's reinstatement and massive expansion of the Global Gag Rule, which withholds funding from foreign organizations that provide or promote abortion, will likely result in at least 2.1 million unsafe abortions and 20,000 maternal deaths.

Unfortunately, the Trump Administration has rejected the longstanding bipartisan understanding of and commitment to U.S. investments in Africa, beyond the security realm. President Trump has met with Egyptian President Abdel Fattah el-Sisi, and spoken with Nigerian President Muhammadu Buhari, South African President Jacob Zuma, and Kenyan President Uhuru Kenyatta. However, these conversations mainly focused on counterterrorism, and neglected the relevant U.S. development partnerships and government initiatives. Trump's Muslim bans were not a reassuring message to the more than 300 million Muslims in Africa. His administration's FY 2018 budget request proposes a draconian 31 percent cut to U.S. development and diplomacy programs, which would disproportionately affect Africa and likely result in the closing of more than 30 U.S. Agency for International Development (USAID) missions.

The United States has critical national security concerns in several African countries currently struggling with protracted conflicts or violent extremist groups that foster instability and hinder growth and development objectives. Nations including the Democratic Republic of the Congo, Niger, Central African Republic, Cameroon, Uganda, and others suffer from the presence of armed rebel groups and terrorist organizations that thrive on vicious cycles of ethnic division, extreme poverty, and poor governance. Since 2006, U.S. Africa Command (AFRICOM) has managed U.S. military operations in Africa, aiming to address the threat posed by groups like al-Shabaab, Boko Haram, the Islamic State, and al Qaeda in the Islamic Maghreb (AQIM).

At present, nearly 19 million people are on the brink of famine in South Sudan, Somalia, and Nigeria, and approximately 14 million people are facing food insecurity in the Horn of Africa – Somalia, Ethiopia, and Kenya. The United States has long been the top bilateral donor of emergency humanitarian and disaster assistance in Africa and the greatest contributor to United Nations peacekeeping operations, the majority of which are located in Africa. Nevertheless, the Trump Administration's withdrawal from development and climate change initiatives threaten hallmarks of U.S. global leadership.

Trump's drastic cuts to U.S. development and diplomacy efforts would stop these programs in their tracks and reverse decades of U.S. investment and relationship building in African countries. Such a dramatic retreat would undoubtedly leave a vacuum and we have already witnessed who will fill it. China has wasted no time in seizing economic opportunities and strategic alliances in Africa. Sino-African trade increased fortyfold in the past 20 years, and China surpassed the United States as Africa's largest trade partner in 2009. As Washington is withdrawing its diplomatic presence and foreign assistance, China is sending its cash and laborers to seize natural resources and build infrastructure with no strings attached.

The hard truth is that when the United States does not act as a forceful advocate for our values and our interests abroad, we leave a vacuum. When U.S. leadership retreats, adversaries who do not share our interests and values fill the vacuum and instability rises. I look forward to hearing from our witnesses on how the United States can protect our varied interests in Africa by building on our accomplishments, meeting security and development challenges, and seizing the opportunities inherent in U.S.-Africa relations.

www.ingramcontent.com/pod-product-compliance
Lightning Source LLC
Chambersburg PA
CBHW081238250726
48654CB00012B/1376